CAPITALIST
DEMOCRACY
IN BRITAIN

Capitalist Democracy in Britain

Ralph Miliband

OXFORD UNIVERSITY PRESS
1982

Oxford University Press, Walton Street, Oxford OX2 6DP
London Glasgow New York Toronto
Delhi Bombay Calcutta Madras Karachi
Kuala Lumpur Singapore Hong Kong Tokyo
Nairobi Dar es Salaam Cape Town
Melbourne Auckland
and associates in
Beirut Berlin Ibadan Mexico City Nicosia

Published in the United States by
Oxford University Press, New York

British Library Cataloguing in Publication Data
Miliband, Ralph
Capitalist democracy in Britain.
1. Democracy   2. Great Britain – Politics and
government – 19th century   3. Great Britain –
Politics and government – 20th century
I. Title
321.8'0941   JN234
ISBN 0-19-827445-9

Library of Congress Cataloging in Publication Data
Miliband, Ralph.
Capitalist democracy in Britain.
Includes index.
1. Great Britain – Politics and government.
2. Political participation – Great Britain.   3. Social
classes – Great Britain.   I. Title.
JN234 1982.M54   320.941   82-14103
ISBN 0-19-827445-9

Set by Hope Services, Abingdon, Oxon
and printed in Great Britain by
Billings and Sons Limited.
London and Worcester

PREFACE

This is a book about the British political system, but my purpose is not to present a detailed description of its different parts. There are many books which do this very competently. On the other hand, there is very little work on the subject which gives due attention — or any attention — to what I believe to have been one of the main threads in the political system ever since the extension of the suffrage in 1867: this is the concern of the people in charge of affairs to contain and reduce popular pressure, in a context which gave to that pressure new opportunities for organized expression.

I try to show in this book that the different elements of the British political system constitute a system of containment; and I think that the nature and function of these different elements are best understood if they are seen as part of such a system. I have no doubt that this approach needs further theoretical development, and also more detailed empirical work. But I hope that what I present here may help the understanding of the spirit and purpose of the British political system; and that it may encourage further work in this mode.

I am grateful to John Saville, and to Andrew Schuller, of Oxford University Press, for some very useful suggestions. My greatest debt is to my wife, Marion Kozak, for her advice and encouragement. For this, and for much else, this book is dedicated to her.

Of course, the responsibility for the text is mine alone.

April 1982   R. M.

CONTENTS

1. INTRODUCTION

I

By 'capitalist democracy', I mean the political system which has gradually developed in Britain since the passage of the Second Reform Act of 1867, and particularly since the suffrage came to include all adults by virtue of the Acts of 1918 and 1928. This political system is commonly called 'democratic', and the notion that Britain is a 'democracy' is taken as a truth too obvious to be seriously challenged. This begs many large questions: if democracy is defined in terms of popular participation in the determination of policy and popular control over the conduct of affairs, then the British political system is far from democratic; and one of the main theses of the present work is that the political system has served, so far as was possible, to prevent rather than facilitate the exercise of popular power either in the determination of policy or in the conduct of affairs. Democratic claims and political reality do not truly match.

On the other hand, the British political system does incorporate a number of democratic features, which make it possible for 'ordinary people' to make themselves heard, and which compel those in power to take some account of popular concerns and expectations. Indeed, the people in power may find themselves out of it as a result of a shift of opinion as expressed in a general election. This may be of much smaller consequence for the actual structure of power than is alleged or believed; but it may also have substantial policy implications and cannot be dismissed as of no consequence.

The term 'capitalist democracy' is also intended to denote a permanent and fundamental contradiction or tension, in a capitalist society such as Britain, between the promise of popular power, enshrined in universal suffrage, and the curbing or denial of that promise in practice. Democratic institutions and practices provide means of expression and representation to the working class, organised labour, political parties and groups, and other such forms of pressure and challenge from below; but the context provided by capitalism requires that the effect they may have should as far as possible be weakened.

I will argue here that it is a crucial concern of those who run the state and other institutions of power to achieve the containment and reduction of popular pressure. This is not only produced by deliberate

management; it is also generated by habits, traditions, and constraints which make for inertia and acceptance rather than for pressure and conflict. Even so, capitalism, like all other systems of domination, has always required and now more than ever requires the containment of pressure from below; and perhaps the most remarkable feature of British history since the Industrial Revolution is how successfully this containment has been managed. The achievement must be taken to be all the more remarkable when it is recalled that enormously disruptive economic and social transformations occurred during this period, and that Britain remained throughout an exceedingly unequal and class-divided country.

There is an obvious sense in which this British record is not unique: other capitalist countries have also successfully contained pressure and conflict. But in no other major capitalist country has this been achieved quite so smoothly and effectively. This is in no way to minimize the degree to which repression and the threat of repression have been part of the containment of pressure: coercion by the state has been an essential element in the achievement of consent in society. But it is nevertheless also true that, in comparison with all other major capitalist countries, power and privilege in Britain have been enjoyed by some, and accepted by the majority, in conditions of relative but quite remarkable social peace. A mere glance at the way in which Britain has ruled Ireland, and in which it continues to rule Northern Ireland, marks the contrast between success and failure in the management and containment of conflict. My purpose in this book is to explore the contribution which the political system has made to the achievement of this high measure of social and political stability in Britain.

It may be said that the people in charge of affairs have had many other purposes and aims — the fostering of economic growth, the security of the realm, the achievement and defence of imperial gains, financial stability, social reform, and so on; and also the advancement of their own careers, the enhancement of their reputations, achieving office, and staying in office. But all such aims have in one way or another been closely related to the task of containing pressure and managing conflict. Social reform, for instance, has been advocated and carried out for many different reasons; but one major reason for it, which does not exclude any other, has been the hope that it would blunt the sharpness of conflict and contribute to the achievement of social stability.[1] Similarly, people who favoured expansion overseas

[1] Winston Churchill provides an apt illustration of the point in relation to social insurance. As Chancellor of the Exchequer in 1925, he received a deputation

hoped that it would, among other things, achieve the same purpose by the promotion of national prosperity.[2] All things considered, it is no exaggeration to say that it is the wish to contain pressure from below which provides the key to the nature and spirit of the British political system: all else depends upon it.

This is not to say that the rulers of Britain have been constantly haunted by the fear of social revolution. There have been times when such a fear has been fairly pronounced: the 1790s and the years immediately following the Napoleonic Wars; the early years of Chartism and 1848, the years preceding the First World War and those immediately following it; possibly 1926 and 1931-2; even 1972-4 and the winter of 1978-9. But what is generally found for the most part is something much more diffuse and less dramatic – a sense of potential danger, the consciousness of a threat which might not be immediately pressing but which could quite quickly become very real. After the great Conservative defeat of 1880, Lord Salisbury, who was not given to wild exaggeration, wrote to his nephew, Arthur Balfour, that what he called 'the hurricane' seemed to him to betoken 'some definite desire for change; and means business'. 'It may disappear as rapidly as it came,' he added, 'or it may be the beginning of a serious war of classes.'[3] This sense of a possible 'serious war of classes' has been a central if not always explicit element in British politics; and it was given enormously greater strength by the Bolshevik Revolution and the fear that Communism might spread further. From then onwards, one of the major aims of all significant

---

of employers' organizations which warned that the incidence of insurance schemes was beginning to impair the national character and undermine thrift and self-reliance. 'I feel', Churchill replied, 'that the system of insurance, whatever may be the effects on the self-reliance of the individual, is going to be an absolutely inseparable element in our social life and eventually must have the effect of attaching the mind of the people, although their language and mood in many cases may not seem to indicate it. It must lead to the stability and order of the general structure' (M. Gilbert, *W. S. Churchill. 1922-1939* (1976), v. 108). Churchill also wrote to King George V that national insurance gave 'millions of people a stake in the country which they will have created largely by their own contributory efforts' (ibid., p. 111).

[2] For a classical expression of such a hope, which Lenin quotes in his *Imperialism, the Highest Stage of Capitalism* (1915), note the words of Cecil Rhodes in 1895: 'My cherished idea is a solution for the social problem, i.e. in order to save the 40,000,000 inhabitants of the United Kingdom from a bloody civil war, we colonial statesmen must acquire new lands to settle the surplus population, to provide new markets for the goods produced in the factories and mines. The Empire, as I have always said, is a bread and butter question. If you want to avoid civil war, you must become imperialists.' (V. I. Lenin, *Selected Works* (1969), p. 225.)

[3] R. R. James, *Lord Randolph Churchill* (1959), p. 72.

political figures in Britain has been to contain class conflict. Where occasion appeared to demand it, there was no lack of will to fight and win; but much the preferred course was to try and avoid violent confrontation. Representative institutions, universal suffrage, trade unions, a party of labour could, for this purpose, serve a more useful function than might at first sight appear: no doubt, they could be viewed as so many weapons in the hands of the working class for the waging of class struggle and the exercise of pressure; but it was perceived that these democratic forms might also help to channel and reduce pressure and conflict.

For the most part, the real problem for the people in charge of affairs was not the threat of revolution but the need, as they saw it, to contain pressure for reforms which 'the nation' could not afford. It was not only necessary to deal with pressure which might pose a major challenge to the system; but also with demands of a less threatening kind. It was neither possible nor desirable to oppose all demands for reform; but rather to reduce as far as possible its cost and scope. The least that was politically feasible was, in this realm, the most that should be done. The political system was well suited to such an approach, for it could easily be turned into an obstacle course from which demands for reform and innovation could be made to emerge suitably slimmed down.

Nor was this concern to limit the scope and cost of reform only confined to Conservative, Liberal, and other such politicians. On the contrary, it is an essential part of the story that Labour ministers have shared that concern. Labour politicians did want reform, and constantly proclaimed their desire to bring about great changes in the social order. But they were readily reconciled in office to the curbing of the reforming zeal they had expressed while in opposition; and they fought with great determination those in the Labour movement who wanted them to do more.

For Conservative and Liberal politicians especially, but also for many Labour ones, the fear of social unrest and even of social upheaval was further strengthened by a feature of the British political culture which has been very marked from the last decades of the nineteenth century onwards, namely a sense of the waning of Britain's brief period of supremacy among the nations, and a sense too of the precariousness of the gains which that supremacy had made possible. In the writings and memoirs of those who have been responsible for the conduct of affairs in the twentieth century there is a frequent sense of decline and danger, even though it is allied to an equally strong will to preserve what could be preserved. In a book published in 1902, R. B. Haldane, later Lord

Haldane, wrote: 'today, at the beginning of the twentieth century, we as a nation have to face the problem of preserving our great commercial position, and with it the great empire which the great men of past generations have won and handed down to us'.[4]

It is not the precise formulation but the sense of a problem of preservation which matters here, and which is typical. Thus, Robert Blake also notes that 'thirty years after Disraeli's Crystal Palace speech when Balfour became Prime Minister in 1902 there was a far greater awareness of the altered position of Britain vis-à-vis her rivals . . . Britain's security, her survival even, were no longer taken for granted.'[5] This awareness grew in subsequent decades, and was reinforced by steady comparative decline. *The Times* rightly summed up this mood when, in looking forward at the end of 1976 to 1977 as the year of the Queen's Silver Jubilee, it said about the previous twenty-five years that 'awareness of national failure, even where it is only relative failure, is acute'.[6]

However, national failure is quite compatible with class success. Class success means the ability of a dominant class to maintain its position in society, and to contain and subdue any challenge to its power and privileges. This is what has happened in Britain. National failure may in time come to threaten class success; but it has not so far had this effect. The question I seek to answer here is 'why not?'

II

Class and class conflict are basic concepts in the present analysis, and require some preliminary discussion.

The vast transformations in British economic and social life to which I have referred are naturally expressed in the changes which have taken place in the British class structure. But these changes have occurred in the composition rather than in the actual existence of two 'fundamental' classes: on the one hand, what is best called a 'dominant class', at the core of which there is the capitalist component, the people who actually control (and who may or may not own) the main means of private economic power; on the other, a subordinate class, mostly made

[4] R. B. Haldane, *Education and Empire* (1902), p. viii.

[5] Robert (Lord) Blake, *The Conservative Party from Peel to Churchill* (1970), p. 169. One historian of conservative disposition, goes as far as to suggest that 'the year 1914 is roughly the point at which it ceased to be fun to be an Englishman' (W. N. Medlicott, *Contemporary England 1914–1964* (1976), p. 79). This may be somewhat overdrawn.

[6] *The Times*, 31 December 1976.

up of the working class, to be more closely defined presently. The nature of these classes has undergone great changes in the last two hundred years, but there are also crucial continuities, in large part based upon the enduring fact of private ownership and control of the main means of economic activity on the one side and the absence of such ownership and control on the other.

From the time of the Industrial Revolution until the last decades of the nineteenth century, the 'capitalist class' could mainly be said to be constituted by a vast scatter of people who owned, or had a substantial share in the ownership of, enterprises which they also controlled and managed. With the ever-greater concentration of units of economic activity, which is a major feature of capitalist enterprise in the twentieth century, a small number of firms have come to occupy a leading and even dominant place in their field of activity;[7] and this is naturally accompanied by a growing 'managerialization' of large firms, with a constantly more pronounced separation of ownership and control, so that those who are in control of vast industrial, financial, and commercial enterprises only own, at the most, a very small part of these enterprises. The owner-controller has by no means disappeared and remains a familiar and important part of the economic (and social and political) scene; but the trend towards concentration and therefore towards 'managerialization' is nevertheless very strong.

There is no need here to enter into the long-standing debate about the significance of the transformations which concentration and the divorce between ownership and control have produced in the capitalist mode of production, and in the character, function, and purposes of the people who run the private sector of the economy. My own view is that these transformations have not brought about any fundamental change in the dynamics of the system; and that it is as legitimate now as it was previously to call the people concerned a 'capitalist class'.

Alongside this capitalist class, there are the people who occupy the top positions in the institutions of the state – leading politicians, top civil servants, the managers of state enterprises, judges, high-ranking military and police chiefs; and to them may also be added a variety of people in the upper reaches of professional life, such as lawyers, accountants, church leaders, and other specialists in communications.

---

[7] See, e.g., S. J. Prais, *The Evolution of Giant Firms in Britain. 1909-1970* (1976). Professor Prais speaks of 'a new world of giant businesses' (p. 1), and of a 'strong trend for concentration to increase, the share of the hundred largest enterprises in manufacturing output having risen from 16 per cent in 1909 to about 41 per cent in 1970' (p. 4). Concentration in Britain, he notes, was greater even than in the United States.

Together, these people control the means of production, the means of persuasion, and the means of coercion. They constitute the 'dominant class' in Britain, the 'ruling class', the 'power elite', the Establishment. It is they who are in charge of the main institutions through which power, responsibility, and influence are mainly exercised; it is also they who, relatedly, make up the higher and the highest brackets of the income scale; and it is among them that most private wealth is vested.

There are of course differences of every sort between the members of this dominant class. Some of the most important of these differences stem from the fact that capitalists and servants of the state fulfil different functions and are subject to different constraints. Capitalists are mainly concerned with their own particular economic domain and are constrained, as capitalists, by the imperative requirements (or by the requirements which they feel to be imperative) of the capital which they control and manage. Ministers, civil servants, and other public servants are required to see further and have different concerns: one of their main functions — perhaps the main one — is so to act as to contain pressure from below, manage class conflict, and maintain the stability of the social system. To do this may require that things be done which are not to the liking of large sections or even the whole of the capitalist class.

Nevertheless, there is a high degree of homogeneity among the members of the dominant class, much of it based on a marked similarity of social background, education, and 'life-styles'. A majority are of middle- and upper-class origin, and have had a public-school and Oxford or Cambridge education. Many of them are linked by ties of kinship.[8] Those among them who started life as outsiders are easily assimilated into the habits of life and thought of the dominant class, not least because such assimilation is an essential requirement for advancement and success in that class. Those who belong to the private sector of economic life find their way or are called into one form or other of public service; and many whose life has been spent in the public service in due course find their way into business. They constantly cross each other's paths in an incessant round of meetings, lunches, dinners, functions, and ceremonies, and as members of boards, commissions, councils, committees, and institutions of the most varied kind.

Most important of all is the very high degree of ideological and political homogeneity which is characteristic of most members of this dominant class. Here too, divisions and differences have always

[8] See, *inter alia*, W. L. Guttsman, *The British Political Elite* (1963); J. Urry and J. Wakeford (eds.), *Power in Britain* (1973), and A. Giddens and P. Stanworth, 'Elites and Privilege', in P. Abrams (ed.), *Work, Urbanism and Inequality* (1978).

abounded; but they have occurred within a relatively narrow spectrum of thought in regard to economic, social, and political issues, and have not precluded a common hostility towards programmes and policies which went beyond gradual, piecemeal, and cautious reform. This was the case throughout the nineteenth century, when the main political division in the country was between Liberals and Conservatives; and it has in practice remained true in the twentieth century, when the main line of division came to be that between Conservative and Labour.

Much, in this connection, has often been made of the various 'fractions' which are said to exist in British capitalism. The existence of such 'fractions' is not to be denied, notably the existence of a 'fraction' of capital constituted by the City, banking, and finance on the one hand, and another constituted by industrial capital. Nor is there any doubt that the former has had a vastly greater influence on economic and financial policy than the latter, as indicated by the closeness of its links with the Bank of England and the Treasury. Nevertheless, a distinction needs to be made here between two separate issues which tend to be confused: the preponderance of financial capital is not in question; but this is not the same as a *conflict* between financial and industrial capital on any serious scale. What is in fact very notable about the existence of such 'fractions' is precisely the absence of any serious conflict between them. As Frank Longstreth notes in a useful survey of this coexistence, 'the articulation of distinct interests has been very circumscribed, mainly in the past by the commitment to the imperial system and the consequent acceptance of the pivotal role of finance in that system'.[9] Factors other than the 'imperial system' could no doubt be added to help account for this acceptance by industrial capital of the preponderance of finance capital, not least the fact that it did not, as industrial capital, suffer unduly from that preponderance.[10] In any case, such economic divisions as there have existed in British capitalism have not manifested themselves in any considerable way in political terms: no 'industrial' party has fought a 'financial' party inside the Conservative Party or elsewhere — or not so as to produce any danger to its cohesion and fundamental unity.

[9] F. Longstreth, 'The City, Industry and the State', in C. Crouch (ed.), *State and Economy in Contemporary Capitalism* (1979), p. 162.

[10] Note also 'the increasing association between financial and industrial capital as City institutions acquired an increasing equity stake in industrial and commercial enterprises, entered the medium- and long-term industrial capital market as well as increasing their consumer credit operations, and provided an expanding range of financial and managerial services' (B. Jessop, 'The Transformation of the State in Post-War Britain', in R. Scase (ed.), *The State in Western Europe* (1980), p. 30).

At a different level, it is also easy to discern a division in Conservatism between, broadly speaking, more right-wing positions and policies and less right-wing ones, or between deeper and lighter shades of blue. This finds expression in all areas of policy, and notably in Conservative attitudes towards trade unions, strikes, law and order, welfare, state intervention in economic life, reform, and repression – in short the strategy and tactics of containment. But the lines of division are often blurred and shifting; and they have never been so profound as to create insurmountable ideological divisions. Conservatism encompasses many tendencies, and is capable of accommodating almost anyone on the right who does not actually advocate a Fascist-type dictatorship in Britain.

The term 'working class' is usually taken mainly to denote manual workers, but this is much too restrictive, particularly in present-day conditions. By now, nearly half the employed population is engaged in non-manual occupations; and most such people, who are employed in clerical, distributive, and 'service' work, are part of what Marx called the 'collective worker' of capitalist society, and are undoubtedly 'working class' (though many of them may reject the ascription). The 'working class' in Britain may therefore be taken to comprise that large majority of workers who are located in the subordinate part of the productive process; and their subordination marks them off from that relatively small part of the 'collective worker' – the directing and managerial element of capitalist society – which belongs to the capitalist class by virtue of its location in the upper reaches of the productive process. The larger part of the working class is employed in the private sector of the economy; but a substantial minority is employed by central and local government, by nationalized industries, and other public bodies.

It is also from the working class that is recruited, so to speak, that part of the population which is in a condition of more or less permanent unemployment and severe deprivation. Most such people are officially acknowledged to be living 'in poverty', together with the poor who are elderly, chronically sick, or disabled. There are millions of them, and they make up a large 'under-class' in British society. The mass unemployment of recent years has added to their numbers, and brought into this 'under-class' young people, particularly black young people, whose prospects of stable employment, let alone skilled employment, are extremely poor.

Like members of the dominant class, members of the working class also have a great deal in common. In addition to their common

subordinate position in the productive process, their income is mostly derived from wages; and the level of their income places them on the lower and lowest rungs of the income scale. The working class shares a common social situation, educational experience, and 'life-style'. Its subordination goes well beyond the productive process: members of the working class individually exercise the least power, responsibility, and influence not only in work but in all areas of society's life. Their only domain of authority — mostly for male adults — has traditionally been the family.

The working class is much more divided than the dominant class. It is divided (and not merely differentiated) in terms of occupation and skill, of sex, race, in some instances religion, often in terms of political perceptions, positions, and choices. There is nothing 'inherent' or ineradicable about these divisions; but they do exist and cut across class lines, oppose worker to worker, and erode or annul class solidarity. This is clearly of the greatest importance in relation to the capacity of the working class to defend itself and to advance its demands. But it cannot be taken to undermine the objective character and the existence of the working class as a social entity whose being is not dependent on the class perceptions (or absence of class perceptions) of those who constitute that class.

There is at any rate no doubt of the quite 'objective' and very large differences that exist between the working class and the dominant class in most aspects of life. Notwithstanding all the propaganda intended to suggest that these differences are mostly a thing of the past, and that 'levelling' and 'egalitarianism' have if anything all but obliterated class lines, the fact is that Britain has always been and remains a very unequal country, in which differences in wealth, income, conditions of work, security, housing, education, and 'life-chances' in general have remained very large, and, at the opposite ends of the scale, truly enormous. Whatever else may be 'democratic' in Britain, the distribution of personal wealth is not, with five per cent of the population owning more than half of total personal wealth, ten per cent owning two-thirds, and twenty per cent owning four-fifths.[11] Nor are the rich for the most part

[11] See, among others, K. Coates and R. Silburn, *Poverty: The Forgotten Englishmen* (1970); H. B. Atkinson, (ed.), *Wealth, Income and Inequality* (1973); D. Wedderburn (ed.), *Poverty, Inequality and Class Structure* (1974); J. Westergaard and H. Resler, *Class in a Capitalist Society. A Study of Contemporary Britain* (1975); P. Townsend, *Poverty in the United Kingdom* (1979); J. H. Goldthorpe, *Mobility and Class Structure* (1979); A. H. Halsey, A. F. Heath, and J. M. Ridge, *Origins and Destinations: Family, Class and Destination in Modern Britain* (1979); and the Reports of the Royal Commission on the Distribution of Income and Wealth, notably the Seventh Report (1979).

'self-made': inheritance has remained the most important single source of wealth inequality.[12]

This does not of course mean that there has been no improvement in the condition of the working class over the years. Manifestly there has, in all areas of life, and not least in the 'relations of production' which govern the manner in which wage-earners encounter their employers. But these improvements do not in the least negate the enduring fact of inequality. Moreover, there is a great deal of hypocrisy in the celebration by the middle and upper classes of the improvements which have occurred in the condition of the working class. For that celebration carefully avoids confronting the fact that most if not all members of the middle and upper classes would experience as intolerable deprivation the style of life and the standard of living of the working class. What is taken to be perfectly reasonable for the latter would be felt as cata- strophically inadequate by the former. Nor can escape from the argument be found by invoking differences of taste. What is at issue here is not Beethoven sonatas as opposed to brass bands, or opera versus soccer, but agreeable as opposed to disagreeable work, a higher income as against a lower one, the good education which the middle and upper classes expect for their children as opposed to the mediocre facilities available to the majority, ample as opposed to cramped housing, greater security as opposed to less or none, and so on. To suggest that these are things which the working class would not really like is not altogether convincing. The claim that Britain, in terms of how life is experienced, is 'one nation', or has been moving towards being 'one nation', is wishful thinking or wilful mystification. There is one nation of large claims on resources, derived from property and high incomes, with privileged circumstances, ease, power, and responsibility; and another nation of wage labour, cramped circumstances, poor prospects, and permanent subordination. The main function of the political system is to maintain and protect these arrangements, and to contain the pressure against them.

However, Britain is more than two nations. Marx had already noted about Britain that 'the stratification of classes does not appear in its pure form. Middle and intermediate strata even here obliterate lines of demarcation everywhere . . .'.[13] Now more than ever, a large and disparate 'intermediate' class exists between the upper and the lower layers of the class structure and helps to obscure the differences between

[12] C. D. Harbury and D. M. W. N. Hitchins, *Inheritance and Wealth Inequality in Britain* (1979) p. 136.
[13] K. Marx, *Capital* (1962 edn.), iii. 862.

them. There are two distinct parts in this class: one of them is engaged in lower managerial, supervisory, technical, teaching, and communications work, and its members are clearly included in the 'collective worker' of capitalist society, but are distinguished from the working class by their qualifications, higher location in the productive process, conditions of work, income, and status. The other part of the 'intermediate' class is constituted by the world of shopkeepers, artisans, craftsmen, petty traders, small businessmen, and other such members of the 'traditional' petty bourgeoisie.

The 'intermediate' class is numerically large, and its salaried part is constantly growing. Both parts of it constitute a strong pole of attraction for the children of the working class, for whom access to the 'intermediate' class represents a substantial achievement of social mobility. On the other hand, the salaried part of the 'intermediate' class has become an important component of the trade union movement; and in so far as its members gain a perception of themselves as a part of the 'collective worker' of capitalist society, they could come to play an important role in class conflict, alongside the working class.

Class inequalities do not by themselves necessarily produce conflict, even though they may exacerbate it. The most basic and enduring cause of class conflict lies in the antagonism which is generated between employer and wage-earner. Here, so to speak, is the primary cell of class conflict, at the 'point of production', from which it extends to many other and larger concerns and grievances. As I have already noted, divisions of every sort in the working class greatly affect the manner in which it presses its demands and wages its struggles. But none of these divisions prevent demands from being made and struggles from being fought. At local, regional, or national level, in one industry or across many, in conditions of greater unity or less, over such issues as wages, hours, and conditions, or for larger economic, social, and political aims, in a multiplicity of different forms, class conflict has been and remains a central and enduring fact of life in Britain; and so therefore has the matter of its containment been an enduring and central concern for employers and the state, and increasingly for the state as an employer.

There is one division in the working class which must be mentioned here: this is the division between the activist minority and the rest of the working class. It is only in very exceptional circumstances that whole classes may be said to have engaged in conflict: thus the British working class may be said to have gone on strike, as a class, in the General Strike of 1926; and the French working class may similarly be said to have gone on strike in 1968. For the most part, however, it is

only a minority of the working class which constitutes its participating, militant, and engaged element. It is this minority which takes part on a more or less regular basis in grass-roots trade union activity, and which is politically involved in the Labour Party and other political organizations of the labour movement.

Not all activists are necessarily very far to the left; many of them in the trade unions and the Labour Party have been content to be the faithful followers of their 'moderate' leaders, and to act as the mainly unquestioning hewers of wood and drawers of water of their organizations. But there have always been many who have been to the left of their leaders, in the trade unions and in the Labour Party, and who have therefore constituted a permanent irritant and challenge to them, never more so than from the sixties onwards.

A certain distance separates working-class activists (and of course other activists) from the bulk of the working class. Stuart Macintyre has made the point well in relation to left activists in the inter-war years:

On the one hand, they were in the forefront of local life, hardworking, respectable, the natural leaders of opinion . . . on the other hand, such individuals were frequently estranged from their fellows by contact with the wider world outside the community, the world of national congresses and conferences, of Ruskin College in Oxford and Central College in London, and the still larger world opened by books . . . this earnest minority, made up of a variety of trade union and labour activists and a sprinkling of Marxists, were at once representative of and strangers in their own society.[14]

How far the same remarks could be made about post-war Britain is an open question. Clearly, some activists occupied positions in politics which 'marginalized' them: but the influence which Communists and other members of left-wing organizations have had in the trade union movement, and for that matter beyond, and which has been out of all proportion to their actual numbers, shows well enough that 'politics' in a narrow sense is only one aspect of the matter. Left activists, generally speaking, have been a crucially important element in the labour movement and in the working class: it is they who have constituted a major generator of radical impulse at the grass roots, and who have been a main means of dissemination of radical ideas and opinions in the working class. They have in this sense been one of the most important

[14] S Macintyre, *A Proletarian Science. Marxism in Britain 1917–1933* (1980), p. 38. Note also his remark that 'the man who attended the Labour College was of course a marked man in the eyes of the management, and was frequently unable to find employment upon his return, but his isolation went further than this' (ibid.).

'counter-hegemonic' forces produced in the British political culture.

In this perspective, it is easy to understand why Conservative leaders (or for that matter Labour ones) should have been deeply concerned with the influence and impact such people might have on the working class. The number of activists might be relatively small; but there has always been the danger that they might none the less succeed in getting the workers to follow their lead.

The actual political and industrial representation of organized labour has not, of course, been provided by grass-roots activists but by professional politicians and organizers, parliamentarians, and trade-union leaders, who have generally been in firm control of policy, and of strategy and tactics as well. At best, the activists have only been able to make a contribution to the shaping of policy. The relationship of the professional representatives of labour to those whom they represent, or for whom they purport to speak, is obviously crucial for the operation of the political system itself, and so is their relationship to the grass-roots activists. These relationships are fraught with great tensions and problems. For the pressures, promptings, and purposes which affect Labour politicians and trade-union leaders are not the same as those which affect activists, or the passive members of organizations of the working class, or the rest of that class. This means that the politics of labour, and class conflict as waged on the side of the working class, involve at least three distinct 'subjects', whose concerns tend to be not only different but may also be contradictory: first, there are those who are in charge of the main institutions of the labour movement (and who may themselves be quite sharply divided); secondly, there are the grass-roots activists; and thirdly, there is the bulk of the working class. Politicians and others who represent the conservative forces in political life have always been very conscious of these divisions in the labour movement, and have quite naturally sought to exploit them.[15] Attempts are constantly made to separate 'reasonable' and 'sensible' leaders from those who are not, and from militant grass-roots activists; and the containment of pressure also requires that these activists should be

[15] 'Conservative forces' is a formulation which will be used frequently in the following pages. It is intended to denote the forces and institutions which serve to oppose, contain, repel, and defeat those forces in society which seek to reform or revolutionize the existing structure of power and privilege. Conservative forces may on occasion seek and implement reform: but reform, least of all in the structure of power and privilege, is not their purpose. Also, institutions whose purpose *is* reform may have a stabilizing effect upon the social order: the Labour Party is a prime example. Nevertheless, it would be arbitrary to list reforming institutions, for all their 'conservative' side, as forming part of the conservative forces. At least, they are not so listed here.

isolated and neutralized. In other words, the divisions in the labour movement greatly and naturally affect the ways in which the class struggle is waged on both sides.

Like the working class, the conservative forces also have their professional representatives in politics, their political activists at local level, and a more or less passive majority of people for whom the politically engaged speak. Here too, there are tensions between leaders and activists. But these tensions in the ranks of the conservative forces are far less marked than in the labour movement, even though the social differences between leaders and activists may be just as great, or even greater. Leaders and activists on the conservative side tend to be fundamentally agreed about their ultimate goals, and generally also about the ways to achieve them. In contrast, both means and ends have often been issues of the most bitter dissension and fundamental disagreement between activists and leaders in the labour movement. Another difference between the two sides is that the conservative forces have many more institutional bases from which they can make their power and influence felt than is the case for the working class and the labour movement. Labour mainly relies on parties and trade unions. The conservative forces have parties and a host of pressure groups, but can also rely on a vast range of agencies which have a greater or lesser impact upon political life and the determination of policy — for instance the press, as well as a great array of 'non-political' institutions and organizations, which are like so many fortresses from which the struggle to defend the social order is waged, not to speak of the state itself. The disparity between the institutional resources of the dominant class and the forces of conservatism on one side, and those that are available to the labour movement on the other, is enormous. Nor is this surprising: it is no more than the expression of the hegemony exercised by the dominant class and the conservative forces.

III

The mode of analysis which I use here, and which accords a central place to the containment of class conflict and pressure from below, has seldom been adopted in relation to the British political system. In the work which has been done in recent decades on British history, class conflict has figured very prominently, largely as a result of the influence of Marxism, with which 'class analysis' is most closely associated. In the realm of government and politics, on the other hand, only a very few books have attempted to present a comprehensive analysis in this mode.

One of them was Harold Laski's *Parliamentary Government in England*, which was published in 1938; another was John Gollan's *The British Political System*, published in 1954; and a third was *The British State*, published in 1958, and consisting of a collection of anonymous essays edited under the pseudonyms of James Harvey and Katherine Hood. It was only some twenty years later, in 1979, that another book was published which was also centrally concerned with class conflict and the political system, though from a very different perspective: this was Keith Middlemas's *Politics in Industrial Society*.

Laski's *Parliamentary Government in England* was a pioneer work, which placed the institutions of the British system of government in their social context, and showed the functions they performed in the defence of class-based society in Britain. However, the book suffered from a basic weakness, namely the pervading notion that the Labour Party's attainment of the role of principal opposition party had dramatically transformed the whole British political scene. This meant, Laski argued, that the two main parties in the state had now come to differ on the 'fundamentals' of the economic and social system in a way that had not been known since the seventeenth century.

The whole political scene in Britain would indeed have been transformed, had the Labour Party in the inter-war years been the socialist party which he wanted it to be, or at least believed that it must soon become. But one of the most significant facts about the British political scene was precisely that the Labour Party was not then, and was not on the way to becoming, such a party. This gave Laski's argument a certain air of unreality, which the passage of time has made even more pronounced. This is a great pity because the argument itself is right: the political system would be fundamentally affected if the Labour Party (or any other party) did become a major force for socialist change; even more so if it was able to form a government and sought to implement a programme of socialist policies. But the fact is that the political system has never had to face such a situation. This of course is something which itself requires explanation.

Notwithstanding its weaknesses, *Parliamentary Government in England* was a remarkable attempt to explain the constitutional and political system in terms that drew much from Marxism; and there is still much to be learnt from it. Had it not been for the war, which changed the perspectives that many people had acquired in the inter-war years, and particularly in the thirties, about the political system and its future,[16] the book might well have opened the way for further

[16] Including Laski's own perspectives. For the change, see his *Reflections on*

work in a similar mode. As it was, the only notable work of Marxist inspiration on the British political system to appear after Laski's was *The British State*. The book had very substantial merits; and there was much about its interpretation of the system which was sharply penetrating. But it was also marred by the application of a rather simplistic and mechanical version of Marxism to the various parts of the British state.[17] In any case, its ideological provenance was then too much out of tune with the ideological bias of most writing on British government and politics to give the book any resonance.

The vast volume of work on the British political system produced since the end of the Second World War was written within a spectrum of thought delimited by mild social-democratic meliorism at one end and a furtively anti-democratic conservatism at the other. The mood of this writing has however undergone some changes over time. In a first phase, which lasted from the end of the war and the election of a Labour Government to the late fifties, the mood was generally self-congratulatory and bland. A new social order, it was widely held, had come into being, or was at least coming into being, and it was much superior to the one it had replaced; and the political system had yet again shown its capacity to absorb and serve the process of change. It had functioned well in the war, emerged intact from it, adapted itself to the 'social revolution' which the Attlee Government was believed to have engineered, and assured just as smoothly the transition from the austerities of Labour in the late forties to the 'affluence' of the fifties under the Conservatives. The two editors of a volume of essays on this period, not notably left-wing, accurately spoke of it as witnessing 'the increasingly active identification of a large and influential segment of the academic community with the forces supporting the status quo'.[18]

This bland mood changed in the early sixties, as the British economy once again began to show signs of severe strain. Reform in the system of government now came to be the theme of innumerable books, pamphlets, and articles — the reform of Parliament, of the civil service, of local government, of the nationalized industries, of the Cabinet, and of everything except the monarchy, and there were even some voices

---

the *Constitution*, which consisted of three lectures delivered at the University of Manchester in February 1950, shortly before his death. The book was published in 1951.

[17] The same applies to John Gollan's much slighter work. Gollan was then General Secretary of the Communist Party.

[18] V. Bogdanor and R. Skidelsky (eds.), *The Age of Affluence 1951-1964* (1970), p. 12.

speaking of the need to 'modernize' this institution as well. Nor did this remain a matter of academic proposals alone: there cannot have been a period when more was done in a shorter time-span to reform different parts of the system than in the sixties and seventies – though to no effect.

From the mid-seventies, the mood changes again: a third type of comment comes to be heard with increasing frequency, which casts great doubts on the viability of the political system itself. In his 1976 Dimbleby Lecture Lord Hailsham, then out of office, declared that 'our constitution is wearing out', and advocated 'nothing less than a written constitution for the United Kingdom'.[19] In a book published in 1977, another writer of conservative persuasion suggested that 'if a nation reveals persistent failure to find a way forward through the tangle of practical problems which it must face, and especially one like Britain, which can look back on a remarkable record of political achievement, there is reason enough for suspecting that it has run into a political impasse . . . the rules governing political life may have lost some of their vitality'.[20] From a different point of the political spectrum, Professor Bernard Crick also suggested, in an essay published in 1976, that 'perhaps for the first time in recent British history, real doubts grow about the adequacy of our political system to adapt itself to social and economic change and to resolve new problems which are seemingly beyond its capacity to control'.[21]

It is not clear what 'adaptation' here means, and to what 'social and economic change' adaptation would be made. In any case, many of the criticisms which are made against the governmental and political system seem misplaced: for what it has been mainly intended to do, namely to keep in being the existing social order and to limit reform, the machine has worked remarkably well. It may not be well adapted to the great changes in economic and social arrangements which Britain does need; but most critics of the system are strongly opposed to such changes.

Keith Middlemas's *Politics in Industrial Society* is much better focused, and his analysis of the purposes which the British political system has served, and has been intended to serve in the twentieth century, makes his book one of the most interesting pieces of writing on the subject in recent years. He starts from the accurate view that the crucial preoccupation of British governments in this century has been

---

[19] Lord Hailsham, 'Elective Dictatorship', in the *Listener*, 21 October 1976, p. 5.
[20] N. Johnson, *In Search of the Constitution* (1977), p. vii.
[21] B. C. Crick, 'Participation and the Future of Government', in J. A. G. Griffith (ed.), *From Policy to Administration* (1976), p. 55.

the avoidance of conflict; and he is concerned to trace two ways in which governments, in his view, have sought to achieve this goal. The first way, he suggests, has been by propaganda, the 'management of opinion in an unending process, using the full educative and coercive power of the state';[22] and his account of this little-explored aspect of the workings of government in Britain is of extraordinary interest. The second way is what he calls the 'triangular pattern of cooperation between government and the two sides of industry',[23] and he describes this as the 'main theme' of his book.

Dr Middlemas is obviously right in stressing that many people in positions of power and influence did nurture a strong 'corporate bias', and hoped that the trade unions could be brought to accept a form of voluntary 'corporatism' which would have made the management of labour a great deal easier. But it seems to me that he overestimates the extent to which this process of incorporation has been carried: one of the notable things about 'industrial relations' in Britain in the twentieth century is precisely that all notions of 'corporatist' collaboration have been very imperfectly realized, and that the trade unions have maintained a large measure of independence. The 'triangular pattern of cooperation' of which Dr Middlemas speaks has no doubt manifested itself in various forms; but the containment of industrial conflict – and of other forms of pressure – has been the result of many other agencies and influences. It is with the most important of these agencies and influences that I am concerned in the following pages.

[22] K. Middlemas, *Politics in Industrial Society. The Experience of the British System since 1911* (1979), p. 19.
[23] Ibid., p. 20.

2. PARLIAMENTARISM

I

By far the most important institution in the British political system is the House of Commons. This might seem an odd view, since there is general agreement that its powers have declined over the years; and whether this is so or not, the House of Commons is not in any case a strong legislative body. Its contribution to the making of policy is generally quite modest, and its control of the executive is on the whole rather weak. In terms such as these, it does not compare well with some other legislative bodies in capitalist democracies, for instance the Congress of the United States.

However, the importance of the House of Commons cannot simply be measured by reference to its strength or weakness in relation to other elements of the constitutional and political system. Its importance does not derive from its actual powers, but from the fact that it enshrines the elective principle and thus provides the absolutely indispensable legitimation for the government of the country; nothing, for the containment and management of pressure from below, could be more important than that.

Legitimation here means that the government exists by virtue of its ability to command a majority in the House of Commons;[1] so long as it is able to do so, it has the right to govern. Whether it necessarily also has the power to govern, to use a vital distinction once made by Marx, is another matter, which is not at issue here. This legitimating capacity, which is the unique prerogative of the House of Commons, turns it into a focus of hope. For it suggests that what is required above all else to bring about fundamental change is a majority in the House of Commons. In other words, there is no need to look for revolutionary alternatives: the mechanism for any change that may be wanted is already available. It is this belief beyond any other which has been at the core of the theory and practice of British government for nearly three hundred years. From the end of the seventeenth century onwards, and on the basis of the struggles of that century, the whole of political life in Britain has been dominated by the belief that the House of Commons was, or could be made to become, the

[1] This does not necessarily mean a majority of seats: a minority government can meet the requirement, though not comfortably or for very long.

effective instrument of such changes as various classes, groups, and interests might at different times want to achieve in the economic, social, and political character of British society.

Nor, for many purposes, was it even deemed necessary to achieve a majority in the House of Commons: a substantial measure of representation or influence would do. For while the House of Commons could not be said to control the government, neither was it merely the pliable instrument of the executive. It possessed a sufficient degree of power to assure its own credibility as an instrument of change; at least, it always had a sufficient degree of power and influence to suggest that it could be turned into an effective means of pressure on the executive.

Belief in the House of Commons as an instrument of change has a basis in historical experience. The first major challenge to the political system inherited from the seventeenth century was produced by the economic and social transformations associated with the Industrial Revolution; the fact that those who were mainly responsible for the challenge were themselves cautious men of property made easier an accommodation between them and the entrenched ruling class. The new men wanted no more than a share of influence and power; and they were as concerned as the old ruling class to contain the radical movements of reform whose demands went much further than theirs. But while it is right to stress how much there was in common between old property and new, this should not obscure the difficulties involved in the political 'restructuring' which occurred in the first half of the nineteenth century, and of which the Reform Act of 1832, for all its extreme limitations, was a major expression and symbol.[2] The important point is that it was the House of Commons which was taken to be the proper arena in which these difficulties should ultimately be resolved.

Macaulay expressed something of this sentiment when he sought to explain why there had been no revolution in England in 1848. Englishmen stood by their government, he said, because:

we knew that though our government was not a perfect Government, it was a good Government, that its fault admitted of peacable and legal

[2] The Act of 1832 only raised the suffrage from some 200,000 to 1,000,000 men; and Professor Hanham has noted that, after its passage, 'landlord influence was, if anything, increased. The counties and many of the boroughs became more than ever the preserves of the great landowners who could command the votes of their tenants. County politics continued down to 1885 to be largely the politics of landlord influence because the law made the tenant dependent upon his landlord. Nor was corruption diminished. If anything, corruption was on the increase after 1832 and it was probably more widespread in 1880, eight years after the passage of the Ballot Act, than at any other time.' (H. J. Hanham, *The Nineteenth Century Constitution 1815-1914* (1969), p. 256.)

remedies, that it had never inflexibly opposed just demands, that we had obtained concessions of inestimable value, not by beating the drum, not by ringing the tocsin, not by tearing up the pavement, not by running to the gunsmiths' shops to search for arms, but by the mere force of reason and public opinion.[3]

It had in fact taken a great deal more than 'the mere force of reason and public opinion' to achieve very partial reform – popular agitation before 1832 for the reform of the suffrage had been crucial in softening the resistance to change. But the point stood that the system admitted of 'peacable and legal remedies'. It was not only the 'respectable' and propertied classes who felt the system to be such: the working class might not think that it was living under a particularly good government, but those members of the working class who were involved in political activity also wanted for the most part to achieve change in the same way. From its beginnings, English working-class politics had a strong constitutionalist and parliamentary bias, and was consciously situated in an ancient tradition of demands for democratic representation within a system already in being. It is, in this context, significant that the charter from which Chartism derived its name as the first authentic mass working-class movement in history should have been a programme for parliamentary reform.[4] Of course, the Chartists wanted much more than parliamentary reform; but it was here, in the achievement of the suffrage, as Dorothy Thompson notes, that was thought to lie 'the primary means of obtaining reform in other fields'.[5] And it was to the House of Commons that, more or less as a matter of course, the Chartists presented their demands for reform.

There did exist a substantial minority, particularly in early Chartism, which was willing to consider and advocate a revolutionary assault upon a political order deemed to be hopelessly corrupt. For some at least, 'the Charter, peacefully if we can, forcibly if we must', was not a hollow slogan. But neither did that slogan exclude the possibility that

[3] Speech of 2 November 1852, in *Works*, viii. 418–19, quoted in Hanham, *Nineteenth Century Constitution*, p. 12. It was also Macaulay, it may be noted, who said that 'universal suffrage would be fatal to all purposes for which government exists', and that it was 'utterly incompatible with the very existence of civilization', which rested on 'the security of property' (Hansard, 3rd series, lxiii. 46).

[4] Namely universal male suffrage from the age of twenty-one; the creation of 300 more or less equal electoral districts; the appointment of triennally-returned electoral officers; the sole qualification for eligibility to be the support of a hundred local electors; annual elections every June; and the payment of a salary of £500 to Members of Parliament.

[5] D. Thompson, *The Early Chartists* (1971), p. 8.

peaceful change might be achieved; and most of the leaders of Chartism were in fact committed to this kind of change and to no other, and one of their main concerns was to curb any tendency there might be to violent actions. They were greatly helped in their endeavours by the fact that there was in being a representative system, whose inadequacies and injustices could be attacked, but whose reform rather than overthrow could plausibly be advocated. Here is the essential ingredient of that parliamentarism which has dominated the political theory and practice of organized labour ever since, and which has been by far the single most important feature of its political existence.

Nothing has weighed more heavily upon labour politics in Britain than the existence of a strong framework of representation: however inadequate and undemocratic it might be, there did exist, it was believed, a solid, proven structure that could be made more adequate and democratic, that had already undergone reform, and that could in due course be used to serve whatever purpose a majority might desire, including the creation of a socialist order. Indeed, my references to a sense of inadequate democracy in the political system may obscure the remarkable complacency with which that system was viewed in the labour movement. In a Fabian tract on democracy, published in 1896, the following reflections are offered:

Democracy, as understood by the Fabian Society, means simply the control of the administration by freely elected representatives of the people . . . When the House of Commons is freed from the veto of the House of Lords and thrown open to candidates from all classes by an effective system of Payment of Representatives and a more rational method of election, the British parliamentary system will be, in the opinion of the Fabian Society, a first-rate practical instrument of democratic government . . . since England now possesses an elaborate democratic State machinery, graduated from the Parish Council or Vestry up to the central Parliament, and elected under a franchise which enables the working-class vote to overwhelm all others, the opposition which exists in the Continental monarchies between the State and the people does not hamper English Socialists.[6]

Such sentiments were widely held in the labour movement, most of all by Labour laders, industrial and political; and they came to be even more strongly held in subsequent decades, when further reforms and greater Labour representation — indeed Labour in office — were realized. This complacency about the democratic nature of the political and constitutional system is all the more remarkable in that, contrary

[6] Hanham, *Nineteenth Century Constitution*, p. 22.

to Fabian assertion, England did not possess an 'elaborate democratic State machinery'. Most of that machinery functioned not according to any democratic or elective principle but on the basis of appointment and co-optation from which democratic pressures and procedures were very carefully excluded. So it has remained until the present; but so too, until very recently, has endured the notion that the British political system was a model of democracy.

Given labour's intense constitutionalism, it was possible to bring it into the political system, and to do so without much or indeed any shock to that system. To speak of this process as the 'integration' of labour is too definite and suggests a greater assimilation than is warranted. 'Inclusion' is a more accurate description of a process that was prolonged and cautious. But labour did enter the political system; and it is useful to identify the main stages of the process, since this illustrates some important aspects of parliamentarism and the workings of the political system.

II

Five stages may be distinguished in the history of labour's relationship to the political system: (i) the period from the late eighteenth century to the Second Reform Act of 1867; (ii) 1867 to the formation of the Labour Representation Committee in 1900; (iii) 1900 to the formation of the first majority Labour Government in 1945; (iv) 1945 to the mid-seventies; and (v) the years since then.

The first period is marked by the more or less total exclusion of the working class from the political process itself, though this does not mean that the working class did not even then constitute a strong presence on the political scene. On the contrary, awareness of this new working class was acute and ever-present among the propertied and professional classes, and so was the fear of what it might do if not kept in check and pacified or repressed. This was a period of intense struggle, in which defence organizations of labour such as trade unions and co-operative societies painfully and gradually came into being, and in which the working class and its activists brought forth a labour movement, engaged in political struggle for elementary economic and political rights. One of its main expressions in the thirties and forties was of course Chartism.

In time, it became ever more difficult to justify the exclusion of the working class — or at least of working-class men — from the political process; and Gladstone was expressing a view that was increasingly held

when he said in the House of Commons in 1864 that 'every man who is not presumably incapacitated by some consideration of personal unfitness or of political danger is morally entitled to come within the pale of the Constistution'.[7] Notwithstanding the qualifications, this signified the virtual severance of the link between citizenship and property. On the other hand, Maurice Cowling is obviously right when he notes that 'neither the Liberal nor the Conservative leaders expected the Act of 1867 to establish a democratic constitution: nor would they have supported it if they had thought it would'.[8] What they did think was that the insertion of part of the working class into the parliamentary and political system, by way of the suffrage, need not represent a threat to the social order; and that it might even turn out to be beneficial to its stability. As Cowling also notes, Gladstone 'sensed the political possibilities of an extended franchise, and the desirability of encouraging a larger share of the population to feel that the centre of its political attention should be in Parliament'.[9] This too was not peculiar to Gladstone. In the context of a solid parliamentary and political system decisively shaped by the forces of property, the extension of the suffrage was more an act of containment than of emancipation.

The Reform Act of 1832 had raised the suffrage to a million people; that of 1867 raised it to two and a half million and left cities and large towns grossly under-represented, with two-thirds of MPs elected by one-quarter of the electorate residing in small boroughs and agricultural areas. Even the Act of 1884 only raised the suffrage to five million, and it was not until 1918 that it was extended to cover the bulk of the adult population with the exception of most women under thirty. It came to include all adults over twenty-one in 1928, though still with many residential and other qualifications, and with remaining elements of plural voting which favoured employers and the well-to-do.[10] The slowness of the process, combined with the fact that it occurred under carefully controlled conditions, was adequately reassuring at every stage. There were always voices to express fear and to urge caution. But the 'leap in the dark' of 1867 was hardly taken impetuously, and the darkness was not very deep; the measures of electoral reform which followed later were even less dramatic.

Even so, the Act of 1867 was of great importance. In the words of one historian, 'it is the crucial Act in that process by which Britain,

---

[7] C. S. Emden, *The People and the Constitution* (1956), p. 3.
[8] M. Cowling, *1867. Disraeli, Gladstone and Revolution* (1967), p. 48.
[9] Ibid., p. 49.
[10] Plural voting was finally brought to an end in 1948.

alone among large European nations, peacefully adjusted her institutions to meet the emergence of a powerful working class'.[11] With the passage of the Act, a second period opens in class relations, in which the problem confronting property and those who spoke for it assumed a new character. The question was no longer how to prevent the working class from entering the political process, but how to ensure that its achievement of the vote should not give it much more weight than hitherto. Richard Shannon has noted, in relation to this period, that 'what worried intelligent ruling class observers was that this mass, by the sheer pressure it exerted, would inevitably transform the entire climate of politics'.[12] 'Intelligent ruling class observers' took seriously the warning which the radical jounalist Henry Labouchere had issued in an article of 1883, and which Sir Henry Maine quoted in a famous book denouncing 'popular government':

Is it imagined that artisans in our great manufacturing towns are so satisfied with their present position that they will hurry to the polls, to register their votes in favour of a system which divides us socially, politically and economically, into classes, and places them at the bottom with hardly a possibility of rising? . . . Is the lot of the agricultural labourer so happy a one that he will cheerfully affix his cross to the name of the man who tells him that it can never be changed for the better? . . . Having forged an instrument for democratic legislation, we shall use it.[13]

The danger was twofold: first, that the working class would exercise undue influence upon the traditional parties; but an even greater danger, secondly, was that it would seek *independent representation*. Walter Bagehot made the point well in his Introduction of 1872 to the second edition of *The English Constitution*: 'A political combination of the lower classes, as such and for their own objects,' he warned, 'is an evil of the first magnitude,' for 'a permanent combination of them would

---

[11] F. B. Smith, *The Making of the Second Reform Bill* (1966), p. 3. However, the extension of the suffrage after 1867 was greatly impeded in practice by registration requirements. With reference to the Third Reform Act of 1884-5, Neal Blewett has noted that 'in 1911, after the system had been in operation for a quarter of a century, some 40% of all adult males were not on the electoral register' (N. Blewett, 'The Franchise in the United Kingdom 1885-1918', in *Past and Present*, no. 32, December 1965, p. 27). 'In some ways,' he also remarks, 'the Franchise Act may be seen as the last of those rearguard actions whereby the Whigs sought to control, direct and dilute the forces of British democracy.' (Ibid., p. 29.)

[12] R. Shannon, *The Crisis of Imperialism. 1865-1915* (1976), p. 221.

[13] H. S. Maine, *Popular Government* (1885), p. 43. Labouchere's article had appeared in the *Fortnightly Review*, 1 March 1883.

make them (now that so many of them have the suffrage) supreme in the country';[14] and he had also said 'what no elected member of Parliament, Conservative or Liberal, can venture to say,' that 'I am exceedingly afraid of the ignorant multitude of the new constituencies'.[15]

The leaders of both traditional parties were themselves determined to keep the new voters within their fold; and in order to achieve this they reshaped their parties and turned them into the country-wide and country-supported organizations which the new politics required. Even before 1867, there had been party organization of a sort in the country at large. But it was after the passage of the Reform Act of 1867 that party-building and the fostering of party allegiances beyond the confines of Westminster were begun in earnest. It was in that same year that the National Union of Conservative and Constitutional Associations was formed, 'primarily to bring together Conservative working men', Professor Hanham observes;[16] and the National Liberal Federation was created in 1877. From the time of the passage of the Act, Professor R. T. Mckenzie also notes, 'the directness and urgency of the Conservative appeal to the working classes is the most striking feature of the early work of the National Union'.[17]

As part of the process of attenuating dangerous tendencies, a momentous change occurs after 1867 in the vocabulary of politics in Britain, with the adoption by politicians of the rhetoric of 'democracy'. It is true that Disraeli, as early as 1835, had claimed that 'the Tory party in this country is the national party; it is the really democratic party of England'.[18] But it was in the decades following the passage of the Act of 1867 that 'democracy' became part of the common coinage of political speech.[19] It was then that politicians came to see the value of appropriating 'democracy' for the British political system. Earlier generations had feared democracy: their successors now proclaimed that it had arrived. Whether the people wanted power or not, they now had it.

[14] W. Bagehot, *The English Constitution* (1928), p. 272.
[15] Ibid., p. 276.
[16] Hanham, *Nineteenth Century Constitution*, p. 228.
[17] R. T. Mckenzie, *British Political Parties* (1963), p. 147.
[18] P. Smith, *Disraeli, Conservatism, and Social Reform* (1967), p. 15.
[19] For a nice example of the indiscriminate use of 'democracy', note the following by Randolph Churchill in the election of 1885: 'The Tory democracy is a democracy which has embraced the principles of the Tory Party. It is a democracy which believes that an hereditary monarchy and hereditary House of Lords are the strongest fortifications which the wisdom of man, illuminated by the experience of centuries, can possibly devise for the protection – not of Whig privilege – but of democratic freedom' (R. R. James, *Lord Randolph Churchill* (1959), pp. 212–13).

The point was to keep power in safe hands while proclaiming that it had passed into the hands of the people. If democracy had arrived, there was no need to agitate for it.

The politicians' appropriation of 'democracy' did not signify their conversion to it: it was rather an attempt to exorcize its effects. In reality, the idea of democracy had made little progress with 'responsible' people. They were reconciled to more and more members of the working class having the vote; and they also agreed that organized labour should be able (within reason, of course) to press its demands upon employers and government. But they thought it absurd and intolerable that ignorant multitudes, quite likely swayed by unprincipled and self-seeking demagogues, should have real power in the making of policy. A carefully limited and suitably controlled measure of 'democracy' was acceptable, and even from some aspects desirable. But anything beyond that was not.

The whole political system was geared to such sentiments; and it has remained much more closely geared to them than political rhetoric would make it appear. Nor have these sentiments pervaded only the political and constitutional realm; they have affected all aspects of life in Britain. Suspicion of democratic procedures, hostility to democratic pressure, the fear of democratic control, are to be found in all parts of society, not excluding the institutions of the labour movement. In this light, the left activists in the labour movement may be seen to have played a vital role over the years in the erosion of the oligarchic features of the state and society. Without them, government would have been even more closed than it is; society would have been even less democratic; civil and political rights would have been even less secure; and the political culture would have been even more impoverished. This does not mean, obviously enough, that everything left activists have said or done has been admirable: but these men and women have greatly helped to civilize Britain.

For the purpose of limiting and controlling democratic tendencies, it was clearly very useful, in the years following the passage of the Second Reform Act, to keep labour politically tethered to the traditional parties; and this was managed with no great difficulty until the end of the century. The Independent Labour Party had been formed in 1893, but it had been unable to secure the support of the trade unions and thus to become the party of organized labour. Other socialist groupings established in the eighties and nineties remained very tiny. But the forces making for the emergence of an organized party of labour were too great to be permanently contained; and the formation

of the Labour Representation Committee in 1900, which became the Labour Party in 1906, ushers in the third period in the history of labour in politics.

That it should have taken so long for organized labour to create its own political party, when it had already long been organized industrially, is a notable proof of the adaptability, resilience, and strength of the traditional parties, and also of the political system which made it possible for these parties to bid with effect for the support of labour. And it also points to the enduring strength of traditional ideas. Many reasons may be adduced for this 'lateness' of labour in creating its own independent means of political representation and pressure. But the existence of a well-established political system, with a proven capacity for reform, must be reckoned to have been a factor of great importance.

The political system also helped to determine the kind of independent political party which organized labour brought into being. There was no break from earlier modes of thought or purpose: on the contrary, it was these earlier modes of thought which dominated the political perspectives of the new organization. The new party was above all a party of the trade unions and of union demands, and not of socialism, even though some of its leaders and members were socialists. The terms on which it was formed, and on which it continued to exist until 1918, represented a deliberate and explicit retreat from the kind of socialist commitment which had inspired the formation of the Independent Labour Party. It was in fact because the leaders of the ILP did not believe that a socialist party would be capable of enlisting the support of the trade union leadership that they helped to create the Labour Representation Committee and the Labour Party. Their own socialist convictions, however deeply held, were loose and flexible; and this made co-operation with non-socialist trade-union leaders easier. That co-operation was further facilitated by the total commitment which both had to the constitutional and parliamentary system and to 'moderate' courses in every respect.

In this perspective, the failure of the traditional parties to avert independent labour representation is hardly dramatic. In no way did it betoken a sharp break with the past. Though the bid to keep labour in the Liberal or Conservative fold was lost, there was yet a gain in the losing, in so far as the new party was from the start eager to work within the political system and had no thought of any radical reshaping of it. As the party of organized labour, the new party was bound to exercise a powerful attraction on socialist activists, the more so since there was no great hindrance within the party to the propagation of

their views. But they did find that they were members of an organization whose leaders had, as one of their main purposes, the containment of their socialist activism; and the Labour leaders did this with considerable success. This came to be even more important after 1918, and it has remained a crucial feature of Labour history.

The whole period from 1900 to 1945 may be seen as one of slow labour development and implantation in the political system at national and local levels; and this also meant the supplanting of the Liberal Party at both levels. It was a gradual process, which only acquired real momentum at the end of the First World War; and it was not until after the Second World War that the Labour Party achieved an implantation that bore any comparison for comprehensiveness and solidity with that of the Conservative Party.

One of the most notable features of this period is the dual perspective in which Conservative and Liberal leaders learnt to see the leaders of the Labour Party. On the one hand, they saw the Labour leaders as political antagonists who must be fought hard. But on the other, they also saw them as allies against 'extremists' in the ranks of labour, whose task must not be made impossible by intransigent and provocative policies and by the refusal to make any concessions to labour's demands. There are many different impulses which move Conservatives to compromise, conciliation, and reform: easing the path of 'moderate' Labour leaders has been one such impulse or calculation. Reform serves many other purposes; but it also helps to reduce militant pressure on Labour leaders.

A good illustration of this concern is provided by the behaviour of Conservative and Liberal leaders when the election of 1923 was found to have returned 191 Labour members (as against 142 in the election of 1922). The Conservatives had 259 seats (as against 347) and the Liberals 159 (as against 117). In terms of seats won and lost, the Conservatives had clearly been defeated. But they were still by far the largest party in the House of Commons, and they had hardly lost anything at all in terms of votes cast, nor in such terms had the Liberal and Labour parties made any significant gains. The claims of Labour to the right to form a government were not compellingly high; and had the other two parties been able to combine, the claims would have been even weaker.

Some of the grounds on which Conservative and Liberal leaders decided that Labour should not be prevented from taking office are interesting. Thus, Asquith told the Liberal Parliamentary Party that 'whoever may be for the time being the incumbents of office, it is we, if we understand our business, who really control the situation . . . If a

Labour Government is ever to be tried in this country, as it will be sooner or later, it could hardly be tried under safer conditions.'[20] Similarly, J. C. C. Davidson, one of the most influential figures in the Conservative Party, wrote that 'I am a simple soul, but any dishonest combination of that sort [i.e. a Conservative-Liberal coalition] which means the sacrificing of principle by both Liberal and Tory to deprive Labour of their constitutional rights – is the first step down the road to revolution.'[21] Neville Chamberlain was of the same mind, and felt that an alliance to keep Labour out of office would only strengthen it for the future, while Labour in office 'would be too weak to do much harm but not too weak to get discredited'.[22] Perhaps the most far-sighted comment was that of Geoffrey Dawson, editor of *The Times*, who wrote to Lord Robert Cecil that 'the safest, as well as the correct, constitutional course is for Baldwin to face Parliament and be beaten. The King would then presumably send for Ramsay MacDonald, who would be unable to govern without Liberal support and would therefore (if he undertook the task at all) gain some experience of administration with his wings clipped.' 'I do not favour this plan', he added, 'with any notion of scoring off the Opposition, but simply because I feel it is the only way in which you will ultimately arrive at a strong, reasonable constitutional party.'[23]

It may be supposed that the leading figures in the Tory and Liberal parties would have tried harder to overcome their differences and their scruples if the advent of a Labour government – even a minority Labour government – had appeared to them to pose any threat to the social fabric, or to anything else of importance. Even so, their calculations and conduct exemplify a high level of 'class consciousness' and political sophistication. The Labour Party was after all pledged to great changes; it took political intelligence to see that it could also be a major

[20] *The Times*, 19 December 1923.
[21] R. R. James, *Memoirs of a Conservative. J. C. C. Davidson's Memoirs and Papers* (1969), p. 189. Davidson's attitude is all the more notable because he had, as Chancellor of the Duchy of Lancaster, been in charge of the arrangements made for dealing with a General Strike, and he was deeply concerned that these should not be touched. He recalled that, on handing over to his Labour successor, Josiah Wedgwood, 'I told him that, whoever was in power, it was his duty to protect the Constitution against a Bolshevik-inspired General Strike. I begged him not to destroy all I had done and not to inform the Cabinet of it. This did not concern party but was a national matter.' When Wedgwood returned the plans to Davidson after the Labour Government had been defeated, the latter also recalled that Wedgwood told him 'I haven't destroyed any of your plans. In fact, I haven't done a bloody thing about them.' (Ibid, p. 180.)
[22] K. Feiling, *The Life of Neville Chamberlain* (1946), p. 111.
[23] J. E. Wrench, *Geoffrey Dawson and Our Times* (1955), p. 224.

force for stability, and that its leaders would be staunch allies rather than opponents in the paramount task of containment of the left, provided their task was not made impossibly difficult. No politician had a stronger sense of this than Stanley Baldwin. His biographer, G. M. Young, has said that:

on the understanding of Labour Baldwin founded his whole policy, in opposition or in office. If the distance between the two parties widened so far that mutual comprehension was impossible, then Parliamentary debate was impossible, and the way was open to actions and reactions, measures and counter-measures outside the scope of the Constitution framed by the experimental wisdom of the ages. Meanwhile, let labour have its chance and learn its lesson.[24]

The Labour leaders for their part played their expected moderating role to perfection. Despite the two brief spells of minority Labour governments of 1924 and 1929-31, and the inclusion of Labour ministers in the coalition governments of the two world wars, the Labour Party in this period was essentially a party of opposition. As such, it played an invaluable part, from the point of view of the conservative forces, in helping the governments of the day to manage the discontents, frustrations and conflicts generated in the inter-war years by relative economic decline, depression, unemployment, and deprivation. These conditions badly required a party which would express grievances and propose remedies; yet one which would also channel and contain pressures, demands, and actions from below. Governments could be relied on to engage in the management of conflict, either by repression or concessions or promises of better times to come. But more was needed, from within labour's own camp, and the Labour leaders supplied it. They were genuinely opposed to much of government policy at home and abroad throughout this period; but they were also totally committed to 'moderate' opposition, and to the neutralization and defeat of any opposition that did not fit this rubric.[25] They thus

[24] G. M. Young, *Stanley Baldwin* (1952), pp. 17-18, quoted in R. T. McKenzie, *British Political Parties* (1963), pp. 121-2. Note also Baldwin's remark on the eve of the General Election of 1924: 'I know I have been criticized, and criticized widely, for being too gentle in my handling of the Labour Party, but I have done it deliberately, because I believe it has been a good thing for this country that that party, comprising as it does so many citizens of this country, should learn by experience what a great responsibility administering an Empire such as ours really is.' (McKenzie, ibid., p. 122.)

[25] Maurice Cowling notes about the years following the First World War that 'social inequality was preserved by collusive collaboration to make rhetoric not action the centre of dispute'; and he also notes that 'in practice conflict divided parliamentary politicians far less than consciousness of the power of parliament

presented the people in effective charge of affairs with enough of a challenge to keep the labour rank and file from seeking different and more dangerous channels of opposition; but not enough of a challenge to deflect the government of the day from carrying out, with only some minor concessions, the policies on which it was determined, at home and abroad.

Whether different Labour attitudes and policies would have made a greater impact on the ways in which governments acted (or did not act) is of course impossible to tell: what is not in doubt is that the Labour leaders made a massive contribution to the containment of conflict in this period. It was, on this score, entirely fitting that the Leader of the Opposition should have been turned into an official personage, with a salary from the state, by the Ministers of the Crown Act of 1937.

In saying that the Labour leaders made a massive contribution to the containment of conflict in those years (but the point applies throughout), I do not mean that there existed vast forces seething with revolutionary anger, which were only prevented from erupting by the endeavours of Labour leaders. There were no such forces; if they had existed, the Labour leaders could not have contained them effectively.

The point is a rather different one. It is that the Labour leaders had a choice of policies and positions, and that they unfailingly chose 'moderate' as opposed to 'radical' courses. They could plausibly argue (though the question is debatable) that ultra-radical policies would have cost them popular support. But it is not very plausible to argue that *any* policies other than 'moderate' ones would have lost them popular support. In other words, they were at all times in a position to choose more radical policies than they did adopt, and they could have expected to achieve at least as much support for those policies as for 'moderate' ones. It is their choice of 'moderate' policies, and their struggles against the more radical policies advocated by left activists inside and outside the Labour Party which constituted their contribution to the politics of containment.

The Labour Party finally achieved a parliamentary majority in 1945; and it is with the achievement of this majority that a fourth period opens, in which Labour moved from being a party of opposition

united them ... from this point of view party must be seen as protecting the classes by persuading the masses to support the parliamentary conflict through which inequality was sustained' (M. Cowling, *The Impact of Labour 1920–1924* (1971), p. 7).

to being a party of government, in office from 1945 to 1951, from 1964 to 1970, and again from 1974 to 1979. It was during the Second World War that a major change occurred in popular perceptions and expectations, and it was of this change that the Labour victory of 1945 was the expression. The war had been proclaimed to be a crusade for democracy against Fascism; and victory against Fascism — in alliance with Communist Russia as well as capitalist but New Deal America — fostered great hopes of democratic advance and radical reform. Many more people than hitherto had come to see that Britain remained an exceedingly class-ridden, unequal, and hierarchical society: all this was now to be changed.

From the beginning, the Labour Government elected in 1945 took it as one of its main tasks to curb these great expectations, and to keep in check the activists, zealots, and 'extremists' who nurtured them. The Labour leaders had strongly opposed proposals for radical policies advanced at the 1944 Labour Party Conference, and had done their best in the course of the following year to narrow the scope and dilute the content of the programme which the Labour Party was to present at the election of 1945. Before that election, Attlee was warning party workers against 'Marxist shibboleths', and K. O. Morgan is right to note that 'in July 1945, Attlee and his cautious colleagues found themselves the unsuspecting, almost the reluctant, legatees of a vast democratic upsurge, unique in British history'; he is also right to add that Labour then failed to grasp 'a rare opportunity to remould a society in flux'.[26] The point, however, is not only that the Labour leaders failed to do more, but that they were able, from the strong position which office gave them, to fight those, in the Labour Party and out, who did want more radical policies. In this at least they were extremely successful, not least because they commanded the unqualified support of the permanently 'moderate' majority of the Parliamentary Labour Party.

No doubt the Labour leaders were helped by the shift of the Conservative Party, or at least of many of its leading figures, towards much more pronounced forms of economic and social interventionism than had been acceptable in the thirties. The shift had occurred in the war years, and was given a great access of strength by the Conservatives' electoral defeat in 1945.[27] Harold Macmillan has recalled the sense that

---

[26] *Times Literary Supplement*, 17 October 1975. These remarks occur in the course of a review of P. Addison, *The Road to 1945* (1975), which analyses Labour's approach to post-war reconstruction.

[27] For the wartime 'conversion' of Conservatism to interventionism, see Addison, *Road to 1945, passim*.

'above all, the party must reconcile itself to the need for a mixed economy and for a synthesis of free enterprise and collectivism. In other words, publicly and privately, I continued to promote the theme of *The Middle Way*.'[28] These sentiments found expression, *inter alia*, in the 'Industrial Charter' which the Conservatives published in 1947, and which, in Macmillan's words, 'proved our determination to maintain full employment, to sustain and improve our social services, and to continue the strategic control of the economy in the hands of the Government, while preserving wherever possible the tactical function of private enterprise'.[29] The document accepted as irreversible the nationalization of coal, railways, and the Bank of England; and it included a 'Workers' Charter' as its final section, whose main theme was 'humanise, not nationalise'.

The shift in Conservative thought and policies did not in the least signify any abandonment of the fundamental objects of Conservatism. It was to strengthen the existing social order, not to weaken it, that the 'middle way' was advocated by its leading Conservative proponents: the 'middle ground' which Conservatives (and others) were urged to occupy was firm Conservative ground.[30] 'Pink' though some 'middle-way', 'One-Nation' Conservatives might then have been thought to be by their more reactionary colleagues and followers, they were in fact part of a venerable Conservative tradition which demanded that minimal concessions be made in order that fundamental advantages be preserved. The real concessions came from the Labour side, whose leaders, with Conservative help, were able to keep to the path of 'moderation', and to keep the left under firm control. It was only in the late seventies that this control became less effective, and this marks the start of the fifth

---

[28] H. Macmillan, *Tides of Fortune 1945-1955* (1969), p. 300. Macmillan's *The Middle Way* was published in 1938. R. A. Butler, one of the main architects of the new policies, recalled that the task was 'to convince a broad spectrum of the electorate, whose minds were scarred by inter-war memories and myths, that we had an alternative policy to Socialism which was viable, efficient and humane, which would release and reward enterprise and initiative but without abandoning social justice or reverting to mass unemployment' (R. A. Butler, *The Art of the Possible* (1971), p. 132).

[29] Ibid., p. 300.

[30] Thus, in a speech at the Conservative Political Centre called 'The Middle Way — 20 Years After' in March 1958, Harold Macmillan, who was then Prime Minister, launched into a virulent denunciation of 'egalitarianism': 'to deny the bold, the strong, the prudent and the clever, the rewards and privileges of exercising their qualities is to enthrone in society the worst and basest of human attributes: envy, jealousy and spite . . . it is only by giving their heads to the strong and the able that we shall ever have the means to provide real protection for the weak and for the old . . .' (A. Sampson, *Macmillan: A Study in Ambiguity* (1967), p. 161).

and present phase of Labour's politics, and with it of a new phase of British politics in general. A discussion of what this involves and portends may be deferred to the last chapter.

It may be noted here that the Labour Party's electoral advances were achieved under a system which greatly distorts the relationship between votes cast and seats won at elections. All representation is to some extent misrepresentation. But there are degrees; and the British 'first past the post' system almost guarantees distortion of the popular vote in terms of party representation in the House of Commons, and on occasion in terms of who forms a government.

In all general elections since 1945 except that of February 1974, one party has obtained an overall majority of seats, though by only the barest of margins in the elections of 1951, 1964, and October 1974. But in no election since 1945 has one party obtained 50 per cent of the votes cast. Yet, government by one party — Conservative or Labour — has been the rule in that period, with the 'winner' claiming a 'mandate' from the 'electorate' for its policies, and with the habitual assertion that 'the British people' had expressed a clear wish for this or that. In the light of what actually happened, this was abuse of language on a grand scale — part of the 'democratic' mythology which forms the most important part of the political culture.

Furthermore, as the Hansard Society Commission on Electoral Reform also noted in 1976, 'in three out of the last thirteen elections (1929, 1951 and February 1974), the party which returned the largest number of M.P's actually had a smaller share of the vote than the runner-up party in the House, so that in a sense the "winner" was in fact the "loser"'.[31] In the General Election of 1951, Labour achieved its highest percentage of the national vote ever, but it 'lost' the election to the Conservatives in terms of seats won, even though they had 200,000 fewer votes. The result was solemnly taken to mean that 'the British people' had decisively repudiated 'socialism',[32] and the Conservatives duly formed a government and remained in office, with further

---

[31] *Report of the Hansard Society Commission on Electoral Reform* (June 1976), p. 9. In its evidence to the Commission, a group called Conservative Action for Electoral Reform noted that 'no single party has ever won a majority of the total electoral vote since the introduction of universal suffrage in 1918' (ibid., p. 9). In the General Election of May 1979, which gave Mrs Thatcher her 'mandate' for great changes in economic and social policy, the Conservative percentage of the vote was 43.9%.

[32] Labour's share of the poll in the borough elections of May 1951 was 55.4%.

electoral victories in 1955 and 1959, for the following thirteen years.[33]

As for individual MPs, it is only a minority of them who receive a majority of the votes actually cast in their constituencies. In many constituencies, the percentage of votes cast for the successful candidate is substantially less than half the number of votes cast. It is only notionally, by convention, and so to speak, as a matter of convenience and courtesy that a Member of Parliament thus elected on a minority vote may be said to 'represent' his or her constituency.

This electoral system has endured despite various promptings for its reform[34] because the two main parties have derived substantial advantages from it. In the case of the Labour Party, there was the hope, from the First World War onwards, that the system would in due course bring a majority Labour government to office; and the minority Labour governments of 1924 and 1929-31 greatly strengthened the attraction and plausibility of such a prospect. For the party's leaders the system had the further advantage of greatly strengthening their hand in relation to their left activists: without 'unity' (mainly on the terms of the leaders), the prospect of office must recede. Nor were Labour activists themselves unmindful of the fact that the system, for all its undemocratic features, indeed because of them, might produce a Labour government; and they naturally believed that a Labour government, whatever might be said against its performance in socialist terms, was better than any alternative.

From the point of view of the Conservative Party, the 'first-past-the-post' system was attractive because it held out the prospect of undiluted majority Conservative rule; and this was indeed the case from 1922 to 1940, with the minor and innocuous interruptions of Labour's tenure of office in 1924 and 1929-31.[35] They also saw the advantage of a system which strengthened 'moderation' in the Labour Party – and which indeed helped them with their own 'extremists'. Even the transformation of the Labour Party into a 'party of government' from 1945 onwards, with the possibility of Labour governments with inflated

[33] 'In the elections from 1945 to 1970 neither of the two major parties ever won less than 39.7% of the national vote, nor won more than 49.3% of it, and on only one occasion during that entire period was the percentage gap between the two greater than 7%. Yet in 1945 Labour's majority was 146, in 1959 the Conservative majority was 100, in 1966 the Labour majority was 97.' (S. E. Finer (ed.), *Adversary Politics and Electoral Reform* (1975), p. 8.)

[34] See, e.g., D. Butler, *The Electoral System in Britain* (1963, 2nd edn.).

[35] The 'National Government' which won the Election of October 1931 was for all practical purposes a Conservative administration, even though MacDonald was Prime Minister. The Coalition Government formed by Churchill in May 1940 was of course predominantly Conservative.

majorities, did not outweigh the advantages of a system which had served Conservatism well for a very long time.

However, the essential condition for its continued acceptability was that Labour, as the alternative party, should remain an essentially 'moderate' party, whose activists should remain under the firm control of its 'moderate' leaders. By the early 1970s, this condition was becoming less assured. The election of February 1974 served to underline a new danger, namely that of a minority Labour government acting as if it had a majority, undertaking the passage of 'controversial' legislation, and preparing the ground for another election soon after the previous one. This is what happened in 1974;[36] and it alerted many people to the defects of a system which they had hitherto found perfectly acceptable. The election of Mrs Thatcher in May 1979 provided some reassurance. But the emergence of the Social Democratic Party as a new political force, with the possibility this portends of 'hung' Parliaments and a minority (Labour) government of uncertain disposition, is likely to produce renewed demands for electoral reform.

III

In conditions of capitalist democracy, with universal suffrage, political competition, and the capacity of the working class to exercise different forms of pressure, the crucial problem for the people in charge of affairs is to be able to get on with the business in hand, without undue interference from below, yet at the same time to provide sufficient opportunities for political participation to place the legitimacy of the system beyond serious question. The point is not to achieve popular exclusion altogether; that would be dangerous and ultimately self-defeating. The point is rather to give adequate and meaningful scope to popular participation; but to 'depopularize' policy-making and to limit strictly the impact of the market-place upon the conduct of affairs. Parliamentarism makes this possible: for it simultaneously enshrines the principle of popular inclusion *and* that of popular exclusion.

The essence of parliamentarism is that it provides a buffer between government and people. It accords to the people the right to elect their representatives and to engage in many forms of political activity; but it

---

[36] In the General Election of February 1974, Labour, with 11,645,616 votes (37.2% of the votes cast) had 301 seats (47.4% of seats); the Conservatives had 11,872,180 (37.9%) and 297 seats (46.8%). The Liberals, with 6,059,519 votes (19.3%) had 14 seats (2.2%). In October 1974, Labour had 11,457,079 votes (39.2%) and 319 seats (50.2%); the Conservatives had 10,462,565 (35.8%) and 277 seats (43.6%). The Liberals had 5,346,704 votes (18.3%) and 13 seats (2.0%).

also bids the people to let their representatives bear the burden of sustaining or opposing the government of the day. It transfers the focus of political life from the country to the House of Commons, and from the people to their representatives: here is where all is ultimately to be decided, sanctioned, endorsed, or rejected. In a strict interpretation of parliamentarism, representatives, once elected, would be allowed to go off to Westminster to attend to their business, and would not be expected to suffer more interference than they themselves thought appropriate, until the next election. Of course, this is too strict an interpretation, in a society where deep strains and antagonisms exist and where capitalist democracy makes their public expression possible. Activists and others will not leave representatives alone. But parliamentarism does nevertheless enshrine a certain division of labour between a relatively small number of professional politicians and those whom they represent. Referring to the extension of the suffrage in Britain, C. S. Emden suggested that:

this kind of development need not raise the apprehension that representative government is in the process of being superseded by direct government. The people's power has not become sufficiently extended to prevent their representatives from using a considerable discretion in the application of the general principles approved by the electors. The representatives retain their responsibility for government. But, in so far as the people acquire the capacity to influence policy, to that extent representative government is modified.[37]

It is certainly true that representative government in Britain has never run the slightest risk of being superseded by direct government. The distance between representative and represented is not fixed in advance; and the British system has always sought to maintain a large distance between them, and to ensure that Members of Parliament were well insulated from grass-roots pressure.

Of course, it has never been prudent for Members of Parliament to offend local susceptibilities, or to do so too blatantly; and they have usually tried not to be too greatly at odds with their active supporters in the constituency. But however much activists (at least in the Labour Party) might wish to 'mandate' their MPs on particular issues, MPs retained, at least in regard to their activists, an almost total measure of independence. There were some very rare occasions when constituency activists were able to get rid of their Member,[38] but MPs could usually

[37] Emden, *People and Constitution*, p. 4.
[38] The most notable example is that of Nigel Nicolson, the Conservative MP for Bournemouth East and Christchurch at the time of the Suez expedition, who

rely on the protection of their party leaders against their constituency parties, at least when it was they who were in line with party policy against the party activists. In particular, a right-wing Labour MP in difficulties with a left-wing constituency party could be sure of support from his or her leaders. Also, MPs who wished to stand again for the same seat at the next election had a virtual guarantee of unopposed reselection. As one writer stated the position in the late fifties, 'it is necessary for Honourable Members to be renominated by their local associations for every election, but they do not have to compete against other potential candidates'.[39]

This has been drastically altered in the Labour Party, where activist pressure in the seventies led to the adoption by the 1979 and 1980 Labour Party conferences of amended selection procedures which exposed Labour MPs to potential competition of a much more serious sort than hitherto, and which thus made reselection rather more problematic. This gives greater influence to activists in the constituencies over their MP, or may do so: the qualification is necessary because it cannot be taken for granted that an MP will in the end have his freedom of action greatly curtailed.

The differences between MPs and their constituency activists are most often ideological and political in nature, particularly in the Labour Party. 'Personal' differences occur, but seldom reach the same pitch of intensity as do differences based on major policy issues or ideological perspectives. Writing in 1867, Bagehot contrasted what he called 'constituency government' with parliamentary government, and argued that the former 'could not be moderate; could not be subject to effectual discussion; could not be in close contact with pressing facts; could not be framed under a chastening sense of near responsibility; could not be formed as those form their opinions who have to act upon them'.[40]

This is obviously a way of stating the difference which is greatly favourable to 'parliamentary democrats' who oppose local activist 'dictation': 'moderate', informed, and responsible judgement is set up against ignorant, thoughtless, and 'extreme' prejudice. But even though this is how the matter has often been presented, particularly in recent

---

incurred the wrath of his constituency party for his opposition to the enterprise. See N. Nicolson, *People and Parliament* (1958), and L. Epstein, 'British M.P.'s and their Local Parties: The Suez Cases' in *American Political Science Review*, liv (2), June 1960.

[39] P. G. Richards, *Honourable Members* (1958), p. 15.
[40] Bagehot, *English Constitution*, p. 127.

years, when the question of the relationship of Labour MPs to their activists has been a matter of bitter contention, the real issue lies elsewhere. At one level, what the greater as opposed to the lesser insulation of MPs does is to help reduce further the impact which constituency activists may hope to have on the political process, by placing yet one more obstacle in their path; and this can only enhance still further the already very sharp separation between the people who belong to the 'political class' and the rest.

Whatever else may be said about it, this separation is not very 'democratic': activist influence at least helps to make the separation less marked. At another level, the greater insulation of Labour MPs from activist influence has had a very specific ideological reach and purpose, namely the protection of Labour MPs from *socialist* pressure. 'Moderate', in Bagehot's formulation, makes the point precisely: it is indeed 'moderation', in opposition to radical pressure, which is in question here. Lofty references to parliamentary democracy and so forth only serve to obscure the crucial issue: will the political system make pressure for radical change more difficult or not? 'Moderate' people naturally tend to favour a version of 'parliamentary democracy' which does make such pressure more difficult.

It is not only right-wing Labour MPs who are at odds with left-wing constituency activists: the whole character of British parliamentarism also makes left-wing parliamentarians vulnerable to pressures and influences which often alienate them from their activist friends and comrades in their constituencies and beyond.

In an earlier era, when Labour MPs were still viewed (and saw themselves) as intruders in the Palace of Westminster, the danger that was thought to threaten them was what Beatrice Webb called the 'aristocratic embrace'; and there were indeed Labour and working-class MPs who were taken up by people in high society, and even by royalty, and who never recovered from the experience. Since those early days, there have been many other kinds of embrace to seduce Labour MPs into greater 'moderation'. But one strong 'conservative' influence is that exercised by the House of Commons itself: left-wing MPs might be immune to all other enticements, but are vulnerable to this one.

Aneurin Bevan has described well what is involved. 'The atmosphere of Parliament,' he wrote, 'its physical arrangements, its procedure, its semi-ecclesiastical ritual . . . are all profoundly intimidating for the products of a board school system who are the bearers of a fiery message from the great industrial constituencies'; and he went on to say that for a new Member of Parliament:

his first impression is that he is in church. The vaulted roofs and stained-glass windows, the rows of statues of great statesmen of the past, the echoing halls, the soft-footed attendants and the whispered conversations, contrast depressingly with the crowded meetings and the clang and clash of hot opinions he has just left behind in his election campaign. Here he is, a tribune of the people, coming to make his voice heard in the seats of power. Instead, it seems he is expected to worship; and the most conservative of all religions — ancestor worship.[41]

Bevan's remarks were based on the experience of working-class MPs in the inter-war years. But even with the changes which have occurred in the texture of British politics and in the composition of the Parliamentary Labour Party since the Second World War, what he wrote is not irrelevant to the attitudes generated by membership of what may no longer be the 'best club in Europe', but which remains nevertheless a flatteringly exclusive one.

However, there are other and far more powerful forces which have traditionally served to foster 'moderation' in Labour's parliamentary ranks. By far the most important of these has been the weight of the party leadership. The independence from the pressure of party activists which has been claimed by and for MPs has simply meant that a different and far more constraining sort of control has dominated their parliamentary existence; and this has worked consistently to keep in check the radical tendencies that might be at large among them.

There are many different reasons why party leaders have been able to exercise a very effective measure of control over their parliamentary troops. One of these is that to follow is generally much less demanding than to rebel, and finds ready justification by reference to something which is held in the highest esteem, namely party loyalty. To rebel is to 'rock the boat'; it is to divide the party and give aid and comfort to the enemy; it is to endanger the chances of the party at the next election. In short, it means behaving very badly in the eyes of those whose good opinion counts. Such behaviour naturally places at risk the chances of office and advancement. For these are in the keeping of the prime minister, as part of the vast amount of patronage which he or she commands; and those who have been disloyal to their party leaders or who have embarassed them can hardly expect to be favoured.[42]

    [41] A. Bevan, *In Place of Fear* (1952), p. 6.
    [42] 'During his two periods at No. 10 Sir Harold personally appointed (or reshuffled) 100 cabinet ministers and 403 non-cabinet ministers, created 243 peers, appointed 24 chairmen of nationalized industries controlling 20 per cent of the nation's gross production, and 16 chairmen of Royal Commissions to administer various policies or make recommendations for future policy, controlled all top-line appointments within the civil service, and, of course, the Honours

The system of patronage extends of course far beyond the prime minister. In 1975, seven cabinet ministers controlled 4,223 jobs; and both ministers and senior civil servants are in effect responsible for the appointment of vast numbers of people to a multitude of 'Quangos' (quasi-autonomous national governmental organizations).[43] It is not very likely that politically 'difficult' or 'controversial' people, i.e. people with strong left-wing views, would often be asked to serve on any such bodies.

Some rebels have managed to beat the system, but only up to a point. The most notable example in this century is of course Winston Churchill. Even though he was a most vocal critic of the Conservative leaders throughout the thirties, and was deeply distrusted as dangerously unsound by many of his fellow Conservatives, he was brought back to office in 1939 and appointed Prime Minister in 1940. But it is worth noting that even at the time when he appeared to be most thoroughly alienated from his party leaders and fellow Conservative parliamentarians, he remained in fact quite close to the centre of affairs, and retained unbroken links with these very same party leaders and parliamentarians. He was not the lonely and peripheral figure which legend has conjured up.[44] And, of crucial importance, no one doubted that he remained a staunch Conservative, wayward of course, but not beyond the pale. Also, Churchill owed his return to office in Chamberlain's Cabinet in 1939 solely to the fact that his opposition to appeasement had been so completely vindicated. It was the war which made him a minister again; and it was disaster in Norway and the imperative needs of war which made him Prime Minister.

There have been other, less dramatic, cases: for instance Bevan, who was not only a critic of his leaders in the late thirties, but who was actually expelled from the Labour Party in 1939, and who maintained throughout the war years a running criticism of the Churchill Coalition Government of which Labour leaders were prominent members. In the climate of thought and feeling engendered by the war, it would have been difficult to keep him out of the Labour Government of 1945, and it was in any case much more prudent to bring him in. He was given the Ministry of Health, an office of great importance, given

---

List.' (T. Benn reviewing Wilson's *The Governance of Britain* in the *Bulletin of the Institute of Workers Control*, no. 33, November 1976, quoted in K. Coates, *Democracy in the Labour Party* (1977), p. 49.)

[43] Ibid., p. 51. For earlier periods, see P. G. Richards, *Patronage in British Government* (1963).

[44] See M. Gilbert, *W. S. Churchill 1922–1939* (1976), vol. v, *passim*.

the decision to establish a National Health Service, but not one of the 'great offices of state'. No politician with strong socialist views has so far ever held any such office. Stafford Cripps, one of Bevan's fellow rebels in the thirties (and a fellow expellee) did become Chancellor of the Exchequer in the Attlee Government, but he had also by then become perfectly safe.

Co-optation is a traditional and common means of dealing with critics and rebels who cannot be brushed aside. It is not politically easy for such people to decline high office (or often not-so-high office) without seeming damagingly awkward; and the temptation is great for the rebel and critic to accept office in the hope of gaining access to the levers of power, to command influence, to cease being the outsider always struggling against a powerful machine. Once in, it is difficult to come out again. In his biography of Aneurin Bevan, Michael Foot recalls that when the Labour Government decided in 1947 to cut the housing programme of which Bevan was in charge — a cut which was part of the general retrenchment that effectively marked the beginning of the Government's retreat into 'consolidation' — Bevan 'had no remedy' short of resignation, and that remedy, he adds, was barred: 'Had he left the Government at that moment, the whole administration might have tottered and he himself would have been blackened as the administrative failure Churchill had always denounced . . . Clearly, resignation would have been folly. Moreover, he believed that the full cuts would never be carried through — and they never were.'[45]

This sort of reasoning, of which there are endless permutations, is the trap in which co-opted erstwhile rebels often allow themselves to be imprisoned and neutralized, at least on the left. In so far as the ideological differences between 'right' and 'left' in the Conservative Party have been much less pronounced than in the Labour Party, co-optation of Conservative rebels has usually demanded from them much less compromise of principle than it has for Labour rebels. For the latter, co-optation has always meant the acceptance and support of policies and strategies which owed very little or nothing to left-wing inspiration. Collective responsibility has required no less from cabinet ministers, or from any other minister for that matter.

Party leaders, at least in the Labour Party, have on many occasions also resorted to severe measures of discipline against their left-wing parliamentary critics and dissidents. In the late thirties, they fought with unremitting zeal any attempt from within their own ranks to

---

[45] M. Foot, *Aneurin Bevan 1945-1960* (1975), p. 93.

organize 'unity' campaigns with the Communists and the ILP against the National Government. They proscribed organizations which advocated such campaigns, including the Socialist League, and thus made membership of such organizations incompatible with membership of the Labour Party. They disaffiliated constituency parties which defied their commands; and expelled MPs and others who proved similarly recalcitrant.[46] Left-wing dissidents were dealt with just as vigorously in the post-war years, when four Labour MPs were expelled from the party, ostensibly for their critical articles and speeches. This was in fact a purging of MPs whose views were thought to be too close to the Communist 'line'.[47] However, one of them, Konni Zilliacus, also had the distinction of being denounced by the Soviet authorities as an agent of Western intelligence agencies, because of his support of Tito after the latter's break with Moscow.[48]

Less drastic penalties were also imposed in this period on other left-wing MPs, such as the withdrawal of the whip, or one-month suspensions from membership of the Parliamentary Labour Party, and with threats of more severe retribution for persistent deviation and dissent.[49] In circumstances where expulsion from the party and denial of the party label meant virtual certainty of electoral defeat, the threats issued by party leaders were extremely effective, the more so because the leaders could be quite assured that they would be supported in whatever they did by the majority of the Parliamentary Party, the National Executive, and Annual Conference.

Having successfully disposed of the 'Communist' issue in the Parliamentary Labour Party, the Labour leaders found themselves confronted in the fifties by the 'Bevanite' challenge to their policies and attitudes. This involved a substantial minority of left-wing Labour MPs, and had a good deal of activist support not only in the constituency parties but also in the trade unions. The movement lacked coherence, determination,

[46] The Socialist League was formed in 1932 to fill the void left in the Labour Party by the departure of the ILP, and had from the start been affiliated to the Labour Party.

[47] R. J. Jackson, *Rebels and Whips* (1968), p. 69. One other Labour MP, Alfred Edwards, was also expelled at the same time for consistent right-wing opposition to official policy. In 1950 he stood as a Conservative and was defeated.

[48] For an account, see K. Zilliacus, *Why I was Expelled* (1949).

[49] Thirty-seven Labour MPs sent a telegram of good wishes to Pietro Nenni, the leader of the Italian Socialist Party allied to the Communists, in April 1948, on the eve of a fateful Italian General Election. This was their offence. Sixteen of the thirty-seven denied that they had actually agreed to have their names appended to the telegram. The remaining twenty-one were required by the party leaders to give a pledge of renewed 'loyalty', and to promise that they would desist from any similar action in the future.

and leadership, and encountered persistent and damaging harassment from the leaders of the Party. But it became increasingly difficult to deal with dissent by the same drastic methods as had been used previously; and in any case Bevanism as a movement soon disintegrated and had for all practical purposes come to naught by the late fifties.[50] The election of Harold Wilson to the leadership of the Labour Party in 1963, following the death of Hugh Gaitskell, created a new situation, in which the Labour left, at least in the Parliamentary Labour Party, was subdued by rhetoric and co-optation rather than by threats and penalties. There was still the occasional expulsion,[51] or the rejection by the National Executive of an 'unsuitable' parliamentary candidate, but the climate of thought in the party and the greater strength of the left made the imposition of sanctions a problematic enterprise. The right and centre remained in control, but their opponents could no longer be bludgeoned into submission.

The control which party leaders have traditionally been able to exercise over their members in Parliament has never been absolute; but it has been very effective in one important respect already noted, namely in reducing the chances of access to high office of persistent rebels and critics. This points to a striking feature of the political system, namely its very effective insulation against people outside the mainstream of political thinking, as defined by the party leaderships. This insulation is not perfect either, but it has worked remarkably well in keeping from high political office people deemed politically unsound. Such people have found the path of advance in political life exceedingly stony, unless they gave adequately convincing evidence of a willingness to rejoin the path of conformity. This too has been particularly effective against left-wing parliamentarians. Nor was there any hope of office to be nurtured outside the main parties. It was on occasion possible for a complete 'outsider' to achieve cabinet office because the prime minister so wished and circumstances so demanded. But this does not affect the point that, while British parliamentarism has had some room for black sheep, particularly repentant black sheep, it has had none for dark horses. Even the break-up of the present two-party system would not, on present form, greatly modify this pattern: the men and women whom it might bring to high office would for the most part be familiar political figures, well in the mainstream of British political life.

[50] See M. Jenkins, *Bevanism. Labour's High Tide: The Cold War and the Democratic Mass Movement* (1979).

[51] For an interesting account of one such expulsion, that of Ken Coates in 1965, see his *The Crisis of British Socialism* (1971), ch. VI.

IV

The left in Britain has generally accepted the legitimacy of the state and the government: so has the right. The labour movement did not for the most part feel it necessary to look further to the left than the Labour Party; and at no time in the modern period have conservative forces felt it necessary to look further to the right than the Conservative Party. In particular, the inability of a British Fascist party to attract the support of any substantial number of people in political life is another and notable token of the solidity of the party and political system in the twentieth century, and is worth probing further.

There were people in the upper classes in the twenties who admired Mussolini and who were in effect Fascists; and there were a good many Conservatives (and others) who admired Mussolini without themselves being Fascists. Winston Churchill can hardly be thought to have expressed his own views alone when he made a resounding declaration to Italian journalists in Rome in 1927 that 'if I had been an Italian, I am sure I would have been wholeheartedly with you from the start to finish in your triumphant struggle against the bestial appetites and passions of Leninism'.[52] But he was no doubt also representative in adding that 'in England we have not yet had to face this danger in the same deadly form. We have our own way of doing things.'[53] This dual view was in fact typical of much conservative thinking then and later: there was much to be said for what Mussolini and Hitler were doing at home, and even abroad (at least until the late thirties); but there was mercifully no need for it in Britain. When Oswald Mosley formed the New Party in 1931, and before it assumed a Fascist mould, there were a number of people, Labour, Liberal, and Conservative, who looked with sympathy upon the venture, because they saw it as an attempt by a bold and impatient former Labour minister to wrench politics out of its apparent stagnation and do something about unemployment and the economic crisis. Even then, there had not been many politicians willing to break with their parties in favour of the New Party;[54] and after Mosley turned the enterprise into an explicitly Fascist organization, he was abandoned

---

[52] Gilbert, *Churchill*, v. 226. [53] Ibid.

[54] Harold Macmillan has recorded that he had been tempted to work with the New Party when it was formed, but had felt that the traditional parties were 'too strongly entrenched' (H. Macmilllan, *Winds of Change 1914-1939* (1966), p. 247). The general secretary of the New Party, Allen Young, became Macmillan's private secretary after he broke with Mosley (ibid., p. 339). The miserable performance of the New Party at the General Election of October 1931, when twenty-two of its twenty-four candidates ended up at the bottom of the poll, and the party's total vote was 33,777, clearly confirmed Macmillan's view.

by the political figures who had at first been attracted.

The Fascist movement was by no means negligible in Britain in the thirties. Press estimates of the membership of the British Union of Fascists in 1934 and 1935 ranged from 17,000 to 35,000.[55] Even the lower figure would be comparatively significant – the Communist Party had 3,000 members in 1931 and it was only in the late thirties that it began to recruit on a substantial scale, achieving a membership of 18,000 in 1938. Dr Benewick has noted that many people in the leadership of the British Union of Fascists had had a public-school, Oxford, or Cambridge background, and that it included a substantial proportion of ex-officers.[56] But it is notable that no one of any prominence in politics was willing actually to make the political leap which joining Mosley involved.

On the other hand, the attitude to Mussolini and Hitler of many members of the Establishment remained one of qualified, or even unqualified, approval throughout the thirties.[57] After all, the dictators were virulently anti-Communist at home and anti-Soviet abroad, which was greatly in their favour; and had they not restored 'order' to their societies, enhanced their countries' place in the world, given them a sense of purpose? When the war came, everybody was required to be staunchly anti-Fascist, and a veil was then and subsequently naturally drawn over the sympathies which the Fascist dictators had enjoyed among people of power and influence in the thirties; but these sympathies need to be noted, not only because they are important in understanding the thirties, but because they are one expression only of what is a permanent part of the political culture, namely the marked indulgence of conservative forces towards authoritarian regimes, however repressive, provided they are suitably right-wing.

Sir John (later Lord) Reith, who exercised legendary power over the BBC for most of the inter-war years (he was in charge of it from 1922 to 1938) provides a good illustration of the pro-Fascist sympathies of influential figures in the thirties. In August 1933, a few months after Hitler's accession to power and the Nazi unleashing of a campaign of terror against their opponents, Reith confided in his diary that 'I have a great admiration for the German way of doing things.'[58] In July 1934, after the Nazi 'night of the long knives', in which the Nazi 'left wing' was exterminated, he wrote that 'I really admire the way

[55] R. Benewick, *Policital Violence and Public Order* (1972), p. 110.
[56] Ibid., pp. 121–2.
[57] See R. Griffiths, *Fellow Travellers of the Right* (1980).
[58] C. Stuart (ed.), *The Reith Diaries* (1975), p. 56.

Hitler has cleaned up what looked like an incipient revolt against him by the Brown Shirt leaders. I really admire the drastic actions taken, which were obviously badly needed.'[59] In November 1935, at the time of the Italian invasion of Ethiopia, he was telling Marconi, who was on a visit to England, that 'I had always admired Mussolini immensely and I had constantly hailed him as the outstanding example of achieving high democratic purpose (*sic*) by means which, though not democratic, were the only possible ones.'[60] And on 10 March 1938 he wrote: 'To a party at the German Embassy by Ribbentrop and wife. I made myself very agreeable to lots of people and quite enjoyed myself. I told Ribbentrop and the Embassy Counsellor to tell Hitler that the B.B.C. was not anti-Nazi.'[61]

More important people than Reith shared his sentiments. King Edward VIII was not only fiercely anti-Soviet and against the left in general; he also nursed warm pro-German sympathies and found nothing much wrong with the Nazis.[62] Nor does it seem that large numbers of 'responsible' people in Britain were greatly outraged by what the Nazis were doing: the struggle against appeasement would not have been so arduous if they had been. Even so determined an anti-appeaser as Churchill could write of Hitler as late as 1935 that he might either bring war or 'go down in history as the man who restored honour and peace of mind to the great Germanic nation and brought it back serene, helpful and strong to the forefront of the European family circle'; and he also thought that the story of Hitler's struggle to 'capture the German heart' could not be read 'without admiration for the courage, the perseverance and the votal force which enabled him to challenge, defy, conciliate, or overcome all the authorities or resistances which barred his path'. But he was also forthright, in the same article, in his condemnation of the Nazi persecution of the Jews and also of the 'proscription' of socialists, communists, trade unionists and liberal intelligentsia.[63] Others were less squeamish, or did not at least allow

---

[59] Ibid., p. 56.   [60] Ibid., p. 57.   [61] Ibid., p. 219.

[62] Mrs Simpson's suspected pro-German sympathies worried the Government, and there were fears that she might see and 'leak' documents destined for the King. 'To combat this, for the first and last time in history papers were screened in the Foreign Office before the red boxes went off to the King.' (F. Donaldson, *Edward VIII* (1974), p. 192). The King was 'against too much slipshod democracy' (ibid., p. 205). After the Abdication, he and the Duchess of Windsor visited Germany, under the aegis of Dr Ley, chief of the Labour Front, and had an amicable interview with Hitler. On the eve of the 1945 General Election he told an American journalist that if Labour won, 'Russia will take over the country in a few days' (ibid., p. 205).

[63] W. S. Churchill, *Great Contemporaries* (1949 edn.), p. 203.

such reservations as they might have to interfere with their expressions
of approval. On a visit to Hitler in November 1937, Lord Halifax, the
Foreign Secretary, told him that

although there was much in the Nazi system that offended British
opinion (treatment of the Church; to perhaps a less extent, the treatment of Jews; treatment of Trade Unions), I was not blind to what he
had done for Germany and to the achievement from his point of view
of keeping Communism out of his country and, as he would feel, of
blocking its passage West. And taking England as a whole, there was a
much greater degree of understanding of all his work on that side than
there had been some time ago.[64]

Indulgence for the Nazis, and even approval of much that they were
doing, was not greatly dimmed by their treatment of the Jews. No
doubt, the Nazis were going too far. But a genteel anti-Semitism pervaded much political and official life; and, like hostility to the left,
helped to blur perceptions of reality. Thus no less a personage than
Neville Chamberlain, the Prime Minister, thought it right to reject
before journalists what was being said about Germany as 'Jewish-
Communist propaganda', and to suggest that 'all these warmongering
stories are got up by Communists, Jewish propagandists and their
sympathisers'.[65]

Such attitudes also help to explain the considerable differences
in the way in which the authorities and the police treated Communists
and Fascists. The former were true evil-doers, the latter misguided
patriots. It was not only Communists who opposed the Fascists in
meetings and counter-demonstrations: anyone on the left who did so
had to reckon with a mainly hostile police and unsympathetic magistrates
and courts.

But as the thirties wore on, many people of conservative views
nevertheless found themselves in the grip of increasingly contradictory
reactions to the Fascist dictators. Such episodes as the victory of
the left in Spain in the elections of February 1936, followed soon
after by the victory of the Popular Front in France, helped to reinforce
a fear and hatred of Communism and Soviet Russia which worked
in favour of the Fascist dictators, including Franco in the Spanish Civil
War. But there was much about the foreign policies of Hitler and
Mussolini which the same people also came to see as dangerous to peace
and to British imperial and national interests. This might not overcome
the will to appeasement; but it raised growing doubts about it. By the

[64] The Earl of Birkenhead, *Halifax* (1966), p. 368.
[65] J. Margach, *The Abuse of Power* (1978), pp. 53, 55.

spring of 1939, after Hitler's occupation of Czechoslovakia, appeasement was on the defensive. There was not nearly as much temptation for Conservatives in Britain as there was for many of their counterparts in France to pose the spurious choice 'Rather Hitler than Stalin', since there had been no Popular Front in Britain to arouse class fears of social upheaval, no occupation of factories as had happened in France, and no other such traumas. There might have been greater fears if the left in Britain had been more effective in the thirties; but it is then also more likely that appeasement itself would not have so strongly prevailed, and that the history of those years would have been very different.

Harold Nicolson wrote in his diary on 6 June 1938: 'We have lost our will-power, since our will-power is divided. People of the governing classes think only of their own fortunes, which means hatred of the Reds. This creates a perfectly artificial but at present most effective secret bond between ourselves and Hitler. Our class interests, on both sides, cut across our national interests.'[66] He was wrong. From the time of Hitler's march into Prague in March 1939, the 'national interest' was increasingly thought to require resistance to German aggression and demands − all the more compellingly as such resistance did not appear to contradict 'class interests'. In the following months, and again in 1940, the House of Commons served as an effective means of registering great shifts of opinion, and this had very large consequences. There was great reluctance on the part of the leading appeasers to make the momentous shift of policy represented by the declaration of war on 3 September 1939. Chamberlain did not willingly give up appeasement: he was forced to do it. As late as the very eve of the declaration of war, on 2 September, he was telling the House of Commons that the Government was still waiting to see if negotiations were possible, and was made to realize that his government would not survive unless he declared war.[67] In May 1940 Chamberlain finally resigned because his support in the House of Commons had been sufficiently eroded at the end of the Narvik debate to amount to a vote of no confidence in his leadership, even though his majority remained very substantial; and his position was further and decisively undermined by the fact that the Labour leaders would not join a coalition government of which he was the head. Their involvement in government was in the circumstances

[66] H. Nicolson, *Diaries and Letters 1930-1939* (1967), p. 342.
[67] In his recollections, Harold Macmillan wrote that Hitler 'could not bring himself to accept that Chamberlain, so malleable before, would prove so obstinate now' (H. Macmillan, *Winds of Change* (1966), p. 602). In fact, the political situation gave him no real choice.

deemed to be essential; but it could not be had with Chamberlain as prime minister. Churchill replaced him because it was not really possible for the other candidate to the succession, Lord Halifax, seriously to claim it, and to be sustained by a House of Commons to which he did not even belong. At this moment of extreme crisis, the political system which had made it possible for governments to pursue with great ease policies that had brought the country to the brink of disaster now served to make possible a major switch in leadership and policies, and to do so moreover in conditions of perfect safety for the conservative forces. The smoothness with which the change was made underlines the resilience and flexibility of the system.

Because Britain was saved by the Channel from suffering the same fate as France, the 'political class' was spared from having to make the choice between resistance to German occupation or collaboration with it. Had it been otherwise, it is reasonable to assume that a British Pétain, Laval, and the rest would have been found to run the government, with the help of the same sort of politicians, military men, civil servants, and others who governed Vichy France. As it was, the political system remained unimpaired through the years of war and was thus able to control and contain the forces of change which were engendered by the experience of war against fascism.

The same point may also be made in relation to later years. Fascism as such was deeply discredited; but Fascist-type organizations such as the National Front were far from negligible quantities in many parts of Britain in the late sixties and seventies,[68] and the sentiments of these organizations on such issues as immigration, the need to 'make Britain great again', and so forth were quite close to those of members of the Conservative Monday Club and many other people in the Conservative Party and beyond it. Nevertheless, such people remained firmly tethered to the traditional framework of politics; and there was no real support in the country for any authoritarian alternative to that traditional framework. It is in this latter respect significant that the most notable figure on the 'populist' Right in the post-war years, namely Mr Enoch Powell, should also have been an ardent parliamentarian and a meticulous constitutionalist. And it may in a similar vein also be noted that the retired military men who achieved a brief notoriety in 1974, when a minority Labour Government came to office, as would-be organizers of anti-strike movements, were also loud in their insistence that they

---

[68] See, e.g., M. Walker, *The National Front* (1977). Mr Walker notes that 'although some 20,000 people went through the NF in 1974, the stable membership was about 12,000 . . .' (p. 9).

were only concerned to support constitutional government against trouble-makers and subversives.

None of this, however, can be taken to provide an accurate reflection of the true strength of extremely reactionary sentiments in the British political culture. On the contrary, subscription to constitutional government and parliamentary democracy tends to disguise, often from the people concerned, how easily commonly-held opinions and sentiments on a large range of issues shade into the authoritarian end of the political spectrum. There are very few people in Britain who would willingly (and publicly) identify themselves as authoritarians. We are all democrats now. But there are nevertheless many perfectly respectable people whose modes of thought have pronounced authoritarian or semi-authoritarian overtones, on the subjects of democracy, trade unions, strikes, militants, sexual deviance, law and order, not to speak of race and immigration. Like M. Jourdain, who did not know that he was speaking prose, there are many people who speak an authoritarian language on many issues, without any particular commitment to authoritarianism – indeed with a commitment to parliamentarism and constitutionalism. These currents of thought run deep, not least through such parts of the state system as the police and the military. How far and in what form they might come to have a greater impact in the future than they have had in the post-war decades will be discussed further in the final chapter.

3. THE CONTAINMENT OF PRESSURE

The smooth functioning of capitalist democracy requires that the working class should accept the general validity and legitimacy of the social order; that it should believe that any grievance or demand that it may have is remediable within the confines and by the traditional procedures of the political system; and that it should also be convinced that any radical change in existing arrangements must be highly detrimental to its best interests.

As for activists who seek to promote radical change, they must be prevented from exercising any marked influence on the working class and the labour movement; and the ideas, doctrines, and beliefs which move them must be relegated to the outer margins of political life, and shunned, rejected, or simply not known by those whom activists seek to influence.

These are difficult and delicate requirements for a capitalist-democratic regime which prides itself on its political and civic freedoms, and which points to these freedoms as proof of its worth. Sheer suppression, in such a regime, is not a possible way of containing left-wing activism. Different mechanisms have to be invoked, which require the involvement of many different institutions. The House of Commons has been one such institution, of crucial importance. But there are many others, without whose contribution the House of Commons could not be so effective. In this chapter I discuss the role which has been played in the mechanism of containment by the main institutions of the labour movement itself, namely the trade unions and the Labour Party; and I then discuss some other institutions which are especially important in the endeavour to contain left-wing activism and pressure from below in general.

I

Trade unions are the most 'natural' institutions of the working class. Workers brought together in a factory by an employer soon begin to seek ways of improving their 'hours, wages, and conditions', and find that this is best achieved collectively. Even so, the strength of employers and the weakness of labour, and other adverse circumstances, often prevent this realization from being translated into union organization. Large numbers of workers are not unionized, in countries where they

are formally at liberty to be in unions. But trade unions have nevertheless long been a prominent feature of the industrial and political landscape in advanced capitalist countries.

Trade Unions are primarily defence organizations. They strive to improve the 'relations of production' which govern the lives of their members at work, seek higher wages, shorter hours, and better conditions for them, and they also act as pressure groups over issues of wider concern, from education and welfare services to defence and foreign policy.

Many writers have stressed the relatively limited scope of trade-union action. Alan Fox, for instance, notes that:

Trade unions strive to effect marginal improvements in the lot of their members and to defend them against arbitrary management action. They do not — and here we come to the crucial point of what issues are *not* at stake in management/worker relations — attack management on such basic principles of the social and industrial framework as private property, the hierarchical nature of the organization, the extreme division of labour, and the massive inequalities of financial reward, status, control and autonomy in work. Neither do they try to secure a foothold in the majority of decisions made within the organization on such issues as management objectives, markets, capital investment, and rate of expansion. Very rarely do they seriously challenge such principles as the treatment of labour as a commodity to be hired, or discarded at management's convenience.[1]

As Perry Anderson has also noted, 'all mature socialist theory since Lenin has started by stressing the insurmountable *limitations* of trade union action in a capitalist society'.[2] However, this emphasis upon limitations should not obscure the fact that the character and scope of trade-union action are not altogether fixed in advance, and that trade-union leaders and others involved in union activity do have some degree of choice in what they do or do not do. This degree of choice can in circumstances of crisis become very large, and fraught with great consequences for labour in general.

Even so, there is no doubt that union leaders and others are subject to very real 'structural constraints', and that these constraints do substantially shape the role they play in a capitalist environment. Trade union leaders and officials are essentially brokers in a bargain between employers who want to buy labour power on the least onerous

[1] A. Fox, 'The Myths of Pluralism and a Radical Alternative', in T. Clarke and L. Clements, *Trade Unions Under Capitalism* (1977), p. 142.
[2] P. Anderson, 'The Limits and Possibilities of Trade Union Action', in ibid., p. 333.

terms possible, and workers who want to sell their labour power on the best possible terms; and in modern conditions they have also often been brokers between labour and the state. They are conciliators, even though they may not see themselves in that role. They are not neutral conciliators as between labour on the one hand and employers and the state on the other: all the same, their purpose is not to promote conflict but to avoid it, or at least to 'routinize' it, to render it more manageable, and to reduce its intensity. Trade-union leaders and officials may initiate strikes, but they do so for the purpose of more effective bargaining, and must seek to bring strikes to an end on what they take to be the best terms available. Having made agreements with their counterparts, they are expected to keep them, and themselves expect to keep them.[3]

This points to one aspect of trade-union activity which has been of great importance in the general functioning of the industrial and political system. Trade unions constitute major institutions of defence — and therefore of attack — against employers and the state. But their role in the process of bargaining and conciliation also and simultaneously tends to turn them into *agencies of containment of struggle*, of crucial importance in the management of class conflict and the subdual of activism.

This is something which governments, for all their attacks on trade unions, have not failed to perceive.[4] It was the emergency produced by the First World War which concentrated ministerial minds upon the need to enlist trade-union co-operation in carrying out the Government's industrial and economic policies and in maintaining industrial

---

[3] It is worth noting that shop stewards are also subject to 'structural constraints'. Referring to their role, the Royal Commission on Trade Union and Employers' Associations (the Donovan Commission) said in 1968 that 'it is often wide of the mark to describe shop stewards as "trouble-makers". Trouble is thrust upon them. In circumstances of this kind they may be striving to bring some order into a chaotic situation, and management may rely heavily on their efforts to do so . . . In addition the shop floor decisions which generally precede unofficial strikes are often taken against the advice of shop stewards. Thus shop stewards are rarely agitators pushing workers towards unconstitutional action . . . quite commonly they are supporters of order exercising a restraining influence on their members in conditions which produce disorder.' (Royal Commission on Trade Unions and Employers' Associations 1965–68, Cmd. 3623, para 110, p. 28.)

[4] In 1886, John Burnett, the first 'Labour Correspondent' at the Board of Trade and himself a former trade-union leader, was expressing the view that 'recent disturbances in this and other countries show very clearly that unorganised labour is most dangerous to social order', and that no stronger barrier to social revolution exists than those which have been erected by the Unions' (J. M. Bellamy and J. Saville (eds.), *Dictionary of Labour Biography* (1974), ii. 74).

discipline.[5] From then onwards, a pattern was set which has been of central importance in the theory and practice of British government: trade-union leaders would have to be relied on to help in the containment of class conflict. At a time of great crisis in 1919, Bonar Law told the Cabinet that 'trade union organisation was the only thing between us and anarchy, and if trade union organisation was against us the position would be hopeless'.[6] The formulation is more dramatic than British cabinets have since then usually found appropriate, but the basic sentiment which it expresses has decisively shaped much of their thinking and strategy: even more than the political leaders of labour, its industrial leaders had to be viewed in a dual perspective, as opponents whose demands and action were often 'unreasonable' and unmindful of the 'national interest', but also as indispensable allies in the management of class conflict.

After the crushing defeat inflicted on the unions by the manner in which trade-union leaders conducted and ended the General Strike of 1926 — a prime example of their contribution to the curbing of class conflict — successive governments until 1939/40 might seek ways and means of institutionalizing trade-union co-operation in securing industrial peace, but they did not have too much to worry about from union militancy: defeat, unemployment, and the preponderance of moderate leaders took care of much of it, and the rest could be dealt with by the government itself. Even so, the unions continued to be involved in a network of co-operation with employers and the state which prevented them from ever developing a sense that they were not an instrinsic and valued part of the social order — and no great secret was made of what they were mainly valued for. The importance which was attached to the contribution of trade-union leaders to the stability of the social order was aptly symbolized by the knighthoods conferred on two of them, Arthur Pugh and Walter Citrine, in the 1935 Birthday Honours List, with a third knighthood bestowed for good measure on the Labour Party's Chief Whip.[7]

---

[5] 'By a policy of shrewd concessions during the war, Lloyd George generally succeeded in involving the official trade union leadership in Government industrial policies, and thereby isolated dissidents among the rank and file' (C. Wrigley, *David Lloyd George and the British Labour Movement* (1976), p. 132).

[6] P. Bagwell, 'The Triple Industrial Alliance 1913–1922', in A. Briggs and J. Saville (eds.), *Essays in Labour History 1886–1923* (1971), p. 106.

[7] This provoked a memorable letter to the *New Statesman* from R. H. Tawney, which denounced the acceptance of 'honours' by Labour people and asked: 'How can followers be Ironsides if leaders are flunkies?'. This was of course based on the (false) assumption that the leaders wanted the followers to be 'Ironsides'. For the full text of the letter, see *New Statesman*, 22 June 1935, and R. H. Tawney, *The Attack and Other Papers* (1953).

The Second World War and its aftermath enormously amplified and accelerated the trend towards involvement and responsibility; and from 1945 onwards, in conditions of more or less permanent economic crisis and relative economic decline, the trade unions were expected, most of all by Labour governments, to play a major part in maintaining industrial discipline, curbing militancy, and persuading their members to reduce their demands for higher wages. This last point has been of particular importance in the attitude of governments to the unions: throughout the post-war years, both Labour governments and to a lesser extent Conservative ones have sought to pursue an 'incomes policy', meaning in effect a curb on wages and not much else, which imperatively required trade-union co-operation.[8]

In seeking this co-operation, governments have been lavish in their tributes to the importance of the role which trade unions now have in society; but they have never failed to couple this with the insistence that, having become an 'estate of the realm' and a great power in the land, the trade unions must also show a due sense of 'responsibility' and support the endeavours of government in whatever the latter were doing. It is significant and symptomatic that it was during a period of mounting economic difficulties in 1961, with the rejection by France of the Macmillan Government's application for membership of the European Economic Community, and an emergency budget in July announcing deflationary measures and a 'pay pause', that was also announced the setting-up of what became the National Economic Development Corporation, in which the Government, industry, the trade unions, and the nationalized industries were to be represented. Its tasks, it was said, would be to 'examine' economic performance, to 'consider' obstacles to greater growth, to 'seek agreement' upon ways of improving economic performance, and so on. Then and at all times, the trade unions found themselves in a position to give advice, in the expectation by governments that this would induce them to co-operate in the implementation of official policies, but not in a position to ensure that the advice would be taken seriously, let alone accepted. As one writer has noted, 'during the discussion preceding the birth of Neddy, many people in the Treasury were highly sceptical about planning; others were resigned to accepting it as the only way of securing union agreement to an incomes policy'.[9] In fact, the 'planning' involved in this and similar exercises was never more than notional: the

[8] See L. Panitch, *Social Democracy and Industrial Militancy. The Labour Party, the Trade Unions and Incomes Policy 1945-1974* (1976).

[9] J. Leruez, *Economic Planning and Politics in Britain* (1975), p. 103.

purpose was not planning but persuading trade-union leaders to co-operate with the Government in the curbing of wage demands.

In the years before the Second World War, it was only infrequently that the trade unions were represented on government committees: the TUC, for instance, was represented on one government committee in 1931 and on twelve by 1939.[10] In the post-war years, by contrast, it was only very infrequently that trade-union leaders and officials were *not* appointed to represent trade unionism on such committees, on the boards of the nationalized industries, on royal commissions, committees of inquiry, and a large number of state bodies from the Manpower Services Commission and the National Enterprise Board to the Advisory, Conciliation, and Arbitration Service and the Commission for Racial Equality. In 1977 it was reckoned that the thirty-eight TUC General Council members accounted for 180 such jobs.[11] But whatever might be said on other counts for this ever-growing involvement of trade-union leaders and officials in the business of the state, it gave them very little influence – and for the most part no influence at all – on actual policy-making; and this was not much less true when a Labour government was in office than when the trade unions confronted a Conservative one.

The trade unions were able to get some wanted measures from Labour governments, and occasionally from the Conservatives.[12] One of the first acts of the 1945 Labour Government was to repeal the restrictive provisions of the Trade Disputes and Trade Unions Act passed after the General Strike. Similarly, in 1964 the Labour Government enacted legislation reversing a judicial decision (Rookes versus Barnard) that had undermined trade-union rights won as early as 1906. In 1974 a Labour Government was responsible for a Trade Union and Labour Relations Act and in 1975 for an Employment Act which widened trade-union rights in areas such as dismissal and redundancy, maternity leave, the provision of time off work to carry out union duties, arbitration, and similar matters. It was also in 1975 that a Redundancy Payment Act was passed. But even though such measures were undoubtedly very valuable, their passage did not mean that trade-union leaders had much influence on the economic policies of the government; in fact, Leo Panitch is right to argue, in relation to the Wilson Government in the mid-sixties, that in fact 'government policies were repeatedly

[10] V. L. Allen, *Militant Trade Unionism* (1966), p. 49; see also K. Coates and T. Topham, *Trade Unions in Britain* (1980), pp. 124 ff.
[11] *Observer*, 7 September 1977.
[12] The Heath Government enacted an Equal Pay Act in 1970.

formed either without first securing the advice of the unions, or after having explicitly rejected their advice. It was not their advice, but their acquiescence and approval which were studiously courted, usually *after* policy decisions were reached.'[13]

The point applies to all Labour governments, and even more so, obviously, to Conservative ones. The reason for this general disregard is that the trade unions do not have the kind of power which is usually attributed to them, particularly in hostile quarters. The belief has been insistently fostered by the media and all conservative forces that the trade unions in Britain have enormous power, greater than that of any other single group in society, greater even than that of government. But this view of trade-union power is not accurate. It is true that trade unions can, in very exceptional circumstances, notably when their own traditional rights are under threat, deploy a degree of power which produces a major crisis. This is what happened in 1968-9 when the Wilson Government sought to curtail the right to strike under the guise of trade-union reform. It happened again under the Heath Government in the winter of 1972-3, when the Government 'took on' the miners, was defeated, and made the mistake of calling an election (which it was in no way obliged to do then), in the hope that it might win at the polls on the issue of 'Who Governs Britain?'. Similarly, union power was also displayed in the 'winter of discontent' of 1978-9, in the major revolt produced by the Callaghan Government's attempt to impose a 5 per cent ceiling on wage increases.

However, these are exceptional cases. In normal circumstances, and in their day-to-day activities, trade unions do not have great power. They have virtually no say in the major decisions of policy which firms take. Nor do they have any real measure of control over the means of economic activity. This is one reason why governments do not have to pay much attention to what they say about economic policy. Both Labour and Conservative governments do listen to industrialists, bankers, and others who do have control; and governments do seek to earn their 'confidence'. Trade unions are by no means helpless as a pressure group upon the state; but the area of their real influence is narrow.

I noted earlier that the degree of power which trade-union leaders exercised was not 'structurally' predetermined: there are many different influences which affect how much trade unions can achieve at any particular moment. One of these influences is that of the ideological dispositions of most trade-union leaders. Of these dispositions, two

[13] L. Panitch, 'The Development of Corporatism in Liberal Democracies', in *Comparative Political Studies* (April 1977), X (1), 80.

may be singled out as having been and as remaining of paramount importance. The first is a wholehearted subscription to that significant motto, coined in the mid-nineteenth century, 'a fair day's work for a fair day's pay'. This is a bargaining cry, not a war cry; and it takes for granted the right of an employer to a share, albeit a 'fair' share, of the surplus: exploitation is not here seen as inherent in the transaction. Also, 'a fair day's work for a fair day's pay' points to the main if not the only preoccupation of those who do the bargaining – wages. To this may be added hours and conditions of work as encompassed in the notion of 'fairness'. Beyond this, there lies a large territory which many trade-union leaders, at least in their capacity as negotiators, have traditionally hesitated to penetrate and explore.[14]

The second ideological influence which has decisively helped to shape the behaviour and attitudes of trade-union leaders is a particular view of what was constitutionally and politically proper, which has had a direct and immediate bearing on their relations with governments and the state and has also affected their negotiations with employers. Trade-union leaders in Britain have very seldom seen the struggles in which they were engaged as part of a larger and more significant contest between capital and labour, and as engagements in a war whose ultimate objective was the replacement of one social system by another. Nor have they doubted the fundamentally democratic nature of the political system and the legitimacy of the state. It is from this view that derives one of the most powerful of the self-denying ordinances which union leaders have imposed upon themselves and their organizations, namely the rejection of 'industrial action for political purposes'. In the General Strike of 1926, union leaders insisted throughout (and may even have believed) that they were merely engaged in an industrial dispute in solidarity with the miners; and they have ever afterwards sought to limit the 'political' reach of the struggles in which they were involved with the state. It has seemed to them perfectly proper to engage in 'pressure group' activity to get a government to change its mind, by way of lobbying, marches, rallies, and other ways of making representations,

---

[14] 'The demands which unions make are based on a concept of fairness which is conditioned by what employers, by and large, are prepared to concede ... The consequence for unions is that their industrial aims have been tailored so as not to disturb the capitalist system or even not to upset unduly any individual employers. Rarely are union demands aimed at altering the ratio between incomes and profits by exploiting whatever market superiority labour may possess. They do not measure each of their acts against the possibility of maximum achievement because the whole range of their expectations is trimmed.' (Allen, *Unionism*, pp. 29–30).

and this could cover any number of issues, including issues of a directly 'political' nature. But strikes are an entirely different matter, and must be strictly confined to industrial disputes. In recent times, this has increasingly involved trade unions in strikes against the state as an employer; but such actions constitute no breach of the self-denying ordinance. Strikes for political purposes, union leaders have always felt, were somehow 'undemocratic', in so far as they were a challenge to a 'democratically elected government'. This has had a considerable effect on the leaders, and hampered them in the deployment of trade-union power. The point is perhaps best underlined by contrasting the attitude of the great majority of union leaders with that of Arthur Scargill in connection with the miners' actions in the winter of 1972–3. Scargill, who was then president of the Yorkshire miners, recalled that:

we took the view that we were in a class war. We were not playing cricket on the village green like they did in '26. We were out to defeat Heath and Heath's policies because we were fighting a government. Anyone who thinks otherwise was living in cloud cuckoo land. We had to declare war on them and the only way you declare war was to attack the vulnerable points. They were the points of energy; the power stations, the coke depots, the coal depots, the points of supply.[15]

This is very unusual language in British 'industrial relations'; it makes many trade-union leaders very uncomfortable; and most of them would probably repudiate it. Their ideology finds expression in much less abrasive language; and is conducive to much less militant behaviour.

There are of course other powerful influences to produce such greater 'moderation'. One of them is the bitter hostility to which militant attitudes and actions are subjected and the barrage of denunciation which they evoke from employers, newspapers, ministers, parliamentarians, and many other sources. Ever since the first Labour Government of 1924, Labour ministers have had a consistent record of hostility to strikes, and have shown great determination in using all the resources of the state in defeating them. The seamen's strike of 1966 led Harold Wilson, the Prime Minister, to denounce the 'tightly knit group of politically motivated men' (i.e. Communists), who were 'now determined to exercise back-stage pressures, forcing great hardship on the members of the unions and their families, and endangering the security of the industry and the economic welfare of the nation'.[16] In the wave of strikes of the winter of 1978–9, Labour parliamentarians joined ministers in a full-throated attack on the strikers, the tenor of which may be

---

[15] *The Times*, 22 November 1979.
[16] P. Foot, *The Politics of Harold Wilson* (1968), p. 175.

gauged from the declaration of the Manifesto Group of Labour MPs accusing the trade unions of allowing 'bloody-mindedness to run riot', and recalling that the Government had a duty to deal with 'anti-social vandalism'.[17]

That 'unreasonable' trade-union demands bear a major share of responsibility (at least) for the ills of the British economy has been one of the main themes of the political culture throughout this century,[18] and has been propagated with unswerving consistency by the daily press, often, in times of great 'industrial unrest', to the point of near-hysteria; and it is worth remarking that there has been hardly any counter-argument in the press against this permanent barrage of attack and denunciation.

Trade-union leaders are naturally affected by it. They are concerned with their own reputation, that of their unions, and of the trade-union movement in general; and they know perfectly well that militancy earns bad marks and 'moderation' good ones. This may not be the decisive factor in shaping behaviour and policies, but it reinforces already well-developed tendencies towards caution; and it also helps to place union leaders on the defensive in the advancement of their demands.[19]

Nor is their involvement in the business of the state irrelevant to the issue. On the contrary, this too is most likely to reinforce the pull towards 'moderation', 'responsibility', 'statesmanship', and other such acclaimed characteristics. Militant trade unionists must run the gauntlet of hostility, denunciation, obloquy, isolation. 'Moderate' ones are assured of praise, public esteem, recognition, 'honours', posts in the gift of governments, an acknowledged role in public life. These are powerful attractions: the wonder is not that trade-union leaders are susceptible to them, but rather that they do not more thoroughly succumb to them.

That they have not is in part at least due to constraints upon them from within their own unions, and notably from the fact of an activist presence that they have had to reckon with. On the one hand, trade-

[17] *Financial Times*, 18 January 1979.

[18] As early as 1901, *The Times* was running a series of articles on 'The Crisis in British Industry' in which 'it blamed Britain's economic decline almost wholly on strikes and restrictive practices' (K. Middlemas, *Politics in Industrial Society* (1979), p. 53).

[19] It is symptomatic of the relative weakness of trade unionism that it should not have a daily paper (apart from the Communist *Morning Star*) to speak for it; and it is equally significant that trade union leaders should not have striven harder to break the virtual monopoly of the capitalist press and to create a contemporary version of the *Daily Herald* (see also below, pp. 84 ff).

union leaders have fought the militant left and kept it under control; on the other, they have only been able to do so by remaining genuine trade-union leaders, engaged, within their own terms and limits, in the defence of their members. They were often valuable allies of the Establishment; but they were not Establishment stooges.

From the time of the formation of the Communist Party, these trade-union leaders waged an unremitting struggle against Communist attempts to influence or gain control of the unions. The TUC occasionally advised unions to declare Communists ineligible for union office; and several unions (for instance the General and Municipal Workers Union in 1928 and the Transport and General Workers Union in 1949) did impose a ban on Communists holding office. But whether under a ban or not, Communists were fought with great determination throughout.

Not all trade-union militants were Communists; but most Communists were militants. This had great advantages for union leaders, because they were able to denounce all militants *as* Communists, or as crypto-Communists, and as agents of Moscow seeking to subvert the unions of which they were members for their own alien and nefarious purposes. However, it must also be noted that 'moderate' union leaders had fought the militants in their unions long before the Communist Party came into being: the main issue was always the demands for militant action and for radical and revolutionary programmes put forward by the left in the unions. It was this that the leaders were above all concerned to combat, as untimely, unnecessary, irresponsible, damaging, self-defeating, and so on. The Communist issue was not unimportant; but it was subsidiary to the issue of militant versus 'moderate' union policies and strategies, whoever pressed militant demands.

The struggles of the trade-union leaders against the left were clearly of immense importance in the containment of industrial unrest over many decades of economic stringency and crisis. Left-wing activists operated in a firmly hierarchical structure, powerfully controlled and regulated by people utterly determined to defeat them; and leaders securely in command had available to them many resources for isolating and defeating left-wing critics and rebels.

The successes which they had against Communists and others would have been less marked if a larger part of the membership of the unions had itself been militant, involved, and 'class-conscious'. But the activists were always in a minority; and far-left activists were always a minority of that minority. The mass of trade unionists was largely passive and ideologically and politically uninvolved, at least after the disastrous

defeat of the labour movement which the ending of the General Strike by the unions' leadership constituted.[20] Trade-union leaders could throughout confidently rely on obtaining endorsement for their policies and positions from their executive bodies and delegate conferences.

Nevertheless, their success was far from total. They were regularly able to defeat the left, but not to expunge its presence from the unions. Communists continued to exercise a degree of local influence out of all proportion to their numbers; and other militants as well remained a permanent irritant to the leaders. This was not only due to their persistence but also to the fact that industrial life and economic conditions never ceased to generate grievances and demands that left-wing activists could take up. Bureaucratic and other constraints reduced pressure, but could not stifle it altogether, even in unpropitious times.

The strong hold which orthodox trade-union leaders had over their own unions and the trade-union movement at large endured well into the fifties. But pressure from below, and changes in the leadership of major trade unions, slowly began to effect a marked shift in union positions. There was no great ideological conversion at the top (or for that matter at the bottom), but rather the replacement in some major unions of the men who had dominated the trade-union movement in the post-war years. Their successors were less fixed in the mould of right-wing Labourism and in Cold War anti-Communism; and they were compelled to respond less negatively to militant pressure and to be less quick to attribute it to the machinations of evil men.

The changes which occurred in the unions in the sixties and seventies, and the greater militancy at the grass-roots, gave new strength to the view traditionally held by governments, Labour as well as Conservative, that the trade unions were one of the main causes of Britain's economic problems, and that this constituted a major political problem as well. Much thought and effort was therefore given to discovering means of at least reducing the problem. One such means was the attempt to tether the unions to an 'incomes policy', either voluntary or compulsory, and under that name or under a less unpopular one. As already noted, the attempt was also made, by both the Wilson and Heath governments, to circumscribe the right to strike and the effectiveness of strike action.

---

[20] The General Strike began on 3 May 1926, at the behest of the General Council of the TUC, in solidarity with the miners' struggle against the coal-owners and the government of Stanley Baldwin. The General Council's call received overwhelming support from organized labour, and that support remained unswerving throughout. Nevertheless, the General Council unconditionally called off the strike on 12 May. For an explanation of their conduct, see R. Miliband, *Parliamentary Socialism. A Study in the Politics of Labour* (1961), ch. V.

This, however, elicited more opposition from the TUC and union leaderships than had been shown at any time since the General Strike, and that opposition even included strike action and the threat of strike action for clearly 'political purposes'. It was a significant token of the new winds that were blowing that even this taboo was then infringed. There were also proposals for the more effective control of plant-level wage bargaining, and for the reduction of the independence of shop stewards; and proposals for 'industrial democracy' which might, it was hoped, induce a greater 'sense of responsibility' in the trade unions.

Nothing that was attempted in these directions came to very much; and one of the main themes of the Conservative Government that was elected in May 1979 was the need to curb 'union power'.[21] But whatever might be said about the unions, the main 'problem', from the point of view of governments, is not that the unions themselves are 'too strong'; but rather that they can no longer be relied on to serve as the same effective agencies of control over their rank and file as they previously did. This means that an important pillar of social stability has become less firm and secure, and this must make more difficult the management of conflict and pressure. It was very convenient to have the unions accept a large share of the responsibility for that management: but if they are no longer able or willing to accept as much of that responsibility as in the past, the state itself is forced to intervene more directly and openly. This produces an unwelcome 'politicization' of 'industrial relations', and creates more likelihood of direct confrontation between the state and the unions.

The Labour Party in the sixties and seventies was greatly affected by the changes which occurred in the unions. Having brought the Labour Party into being, union leaders had until then vigilantly helped its political leaders to keep it on the path of cautious reform, in the belief that this was the only possible and desirable way forward for the labour movement and the working class. There was a fundamental congruence in outlook and aims between the industrial and political 'wings' of the movement; and union leaders were willing and eager to act, in a familiar formulation, as the 'praetorian guard' of the Labour leadership, and to protect it against critics and dissidents on the left with the crushing weight of their block vote at annual conferences of the party.

This congruence came under strain, over such issues as wage restraint, from the sixties onwards; and this was a major contributory cause to

---

[21] Legislation passed since then goes some way in this direction.

what might be called the crisis of containment in the Labour Party in this period.

II

There is in capitalist democracy an endless variety of pressure groups and political organizations, all of them seeking to make an impact on the state, on particular segments of the population, or on society at large. But it is political parties which have traditionally had a particular attraction for political activists at the grass roots. In Britain, the political activism expressed through political parties has been extremely concentrated because of the preponderance of two main parties throughout this century. It has been possible for activists on the right and on the left to find political organizations in which to work other than the Conservative or Labour Party: but it is these two parties which, ever since the twenties, political activists have mainly sought to influence.

On the other hand, party leaders, of both parties, have constantly sought to blunt edges which political activists were keen to sharpen; and given this difference of perception and purpose, those in charge of political parties have tended to view their activists with mixed feelings. In the Labour Party in particular, they could not but welcome and encourage a commitment which ensured the performance, on a voluntary basis, of activities, tasks, and chores, which gave their party a visible presence in the constituencies, and which could not have been ensured in any other way, because of the financial stringencies under which the Labour Party has always had to operate. Grass-roots activists provided the national party with a permanent and fairly solid infrastructure; they acted as 'transmission belts' from the centre to the periphery, gave support to sitting MPs and to parliamentary candidates; and they rendered invaluable service at election time. Both parties are electoral machines, and have generally been more concerned with elections than anything else; and without the contribution of the activists, the electoral machines would be stalled.

Had activists been content to play this purely subordinate role, there would have been no serious reason for mixed feelings about them on the part of their leaders. But activists, or at least some activists, have never been content with a purely supportive role: they have also wanted to influence party policy, even to shape it. This has been much less of a problem in the Conservative Party than in the Labour Party, where it has been central to its political life. Conservative activists are constrained by a much greater sense of deference, loyalty, and submission

to the authority of their leaders than is the case in the Labour Party. Also, they are not expected, in formal constitutional terms, to shape party policy. That power is vested in the Leader; and while activists may hope that the Leader and the leading people in the party will take account of rank and file sentiments expressed at party conferences and other gatherings, they make no claim to any 'sovereign' rights for annual conference.

The most important reason for the effectiveness of these constraints has already been noted: it is that Conservative activists generally tend to feel that they can trust their leaders; and they feel this because their leaders have always tended to reflect the views, beliefs, aspirations, hopes, prejudices, and hatreds of their rank and file. Some — perhaps many — Conservative activists might think that their leaders were too far given to compromise and conciliation, and insufficiently vigorous in defence of the activist version of true Conservatism. But the differences have been of degree, not of kind: there has been no yawning abyss of principle and perspective, no fundamental divide as to what was the ultimate purpose of the Conservative Party.

This cannot be said of the Labour Party. On the contrary, the division between Labour leaders and Labour left activists has been permanent and fundamental, and has not only concerned issues and policies, but the very purpose of the party. This has often been obscured by a conference rhetoric which the leaders of the Labour Party have brought to artistic perfection; but it has nevertheless weighed heavily upon the party throughout its existence.

The pattern has been absolutely consistent: from the very beginning of the Labour Party's history, its leaders have assumed the role of dedicated and indefatigable crusaders against what they judged to be ill-informed, stupid, electorally damaging, and in any case unattainable demands and policies, emanating from constituency parties influenced or run, in Sidney Webb's famous phrase of 1930, by 'unrepresentative groups of nonentities dominated by fanatics and cranks and extremists'.[22]

---

[22] R. T. Mackenzie, *British Political Parties* (1963), p. 506. In *The Future of Socialism*, C. A. R. Crosland expressed an anti-activist bias in rather different terms: 'we surely do not want a world in which everyone is fussing around', he wrote, 'in an interfering and responsible manner, and noone peacefully cultivating his garden . . . one does not necessarily want a busy, bustling society in which everyone is politically active, and spends his evenings in group discussions, and feels responsible for all the burdens of the world' (C. A. R. Crosland, *The Future of Socialism* (1956), p. 341). More precisely, he wrote in 1968 that 'a continuous political activism by the great bulk of the population would . . . pose a real threat to the stability of our democracy' ('Socialists in a Dangerous World', in *Socialist Commentary* Supplement, November 1968, quoted by L. Minkin, *The Labour Party Conference* (1978), p. 277).

There is no record of any Labour Party leaders ever having used their commanding position to press more radical policies on reluctant activists: the trend has always and uniformly been the other way. More power to the leaders has meant less radical policies; and vice versa. Robert Michels wrote that 'it is indisputable that the oligarchical and bureaucratic tendency of party organization is a matter of technical and practical necessity'.[23] But this leaves out of account the matter of ideology, and the fact that the leaders of the Labour Party, bent on one set of policies, have needed to protect themselves from their activists, who were bent on a very different set of policies, and that they naturally sought protection from their activists by concentrating power in the centre and reducing it at the periphery. There are indeed other reasons for the tendency to oligarchy and bureaucracy in large organizations; but that tendency is powerfully reinforced in the Labour Party by the ideological divisions between leaders and activists.

The Labour Party has always been formally committed to democratic internal practices, enshrined in the ultimate sovereignty of annual conference, and its leaders have habitually pointed to the difference which, they claimed, existed in this respect between their party and the Conservatives. In actual fact, Labour leaders, at least until recently, have not had much less power *vis-à-vis* their followers than Conservative ones. In his Introduction to Bagehot's *The English Constitution*, Richard Crossman robustly wrote that:

since it could not afford, like its opponents, to maintain a large army of paid party workers, the Labour Party required militants — politically conscious socialists to do the work of organising the constituencies. But since these militants tended to be 'extremists', a constitution was needed which maintained their enthusiasm by apparently creating a full party democracy while excluding them from effective power. Hence the concession in principle of sovereign powers to the delegates of the Annual Conference, and the removal in practice of most of this sovereignty through the trade union block vote on the one hand, and the complete independence of the Parliamentary Labour Party on the other.[24]

This was indeed how the system worked until recent years. There were occasional victories for the activists, of which by far the most spectacular, achieved under very unusual circumstances, was the victory which the 1944 annual conference scored over the leadership in getting

[23] R. Michels, *Political Parties* (1959), p. 35.
[24] R H. S Crossman, Introduction, in W. Bagehot, *The English Constitution* (1963), p. 41. Sidney Webb's remarks which were quoted earlier also included the view that '*if* the block vote of the Trade Unions were eliminated it would be impracticable to continue to vest the control of policy in Labour Party Conferences' (Mckenzie, *Parties*, p. 506).

adopted the public ownership proposals which later appeared — in a diluted form — in *Let Us Face the Future*, the programme on which Labour fought and won the election of July 1945; and there were other occasions, even at the height of the leadership's preponderance, when activists in the party were able to inflect policy. And it can also be argued that the policies adopted by the leadership would at all times have been even more 'moderate' than they actually were had it not been for the influence which the activists were able to exercise. The fact that they had *some* influence was of the utmost importance in keeping them in the Labour Party. If their leaders had been in total and unqualified control, in such a way as to render any challenge impossible, the activists would have lost heart and the Labour Party would not have been able to keep them in its fold. As it was, such successes as they had nurtured the hope that they would in time wield more influence and even come to control the party.

Meanwhile, the Labour leaders remained in more than adequate control of party policy, and were in secure command of the annual conference, the National Executive Committee, and the Parliamentary Labour Party. Even on the rare occasions when they were defeated at annual conference, they could for the most part safely afford to ignore the resolutions to which they objected. On one famous occasion, when Hugh Gaitskell was defeated on the issue of defence and unilateral nuclear disarmament at the annual conference of 1960, he could, even in anticipation of the adverse vote which he knew was coming, pledge to 'fight and fight and fight again to bring back sanity and honesty and dignity' to the Labour Party, meaning in effect that he would refuse to abide by conference's decision and would seek to reverse it, which he did.[25] Party leaders could also justify their refusal to accept the 'sovereignty' of annual conference by investing the notion with an absurdly literal meaning. Thus, in July 1959, Gaitskell had agreed that 'it is right and proper in this democratic party of ours that we should argue out and settle ultimately in our conference the great issues of policy'; but it was not right, he had gone on to say, 'that a future Labour Government should be committed by Conference decisions one way or the other on every matter of detail for all time'.[26] In the same vein, Harold Wilson said in 1970 that no one would suggest that a government 'operating within the broad strategy, laid down by the Party programme, stemming from Conference, which Conference has asked should be included in the manifesto, should be required automatically

[25] *Labour Party Annual Conference Report, 1960*, p. 201.
[26] Minkin, *Labour Conference*, p. 273.

to carry out each and every decision of each and every Annual Conference'.[27] But activists did not for the most part ask for such a punctilious and detailed observance by their leaders of every conference decision: all they wanted was precisely that their leaders should 'operate within the broad strategy laid down by Party Conference' and seek to act in the spirit of party decisions. Nor was their insistence on the sovereignty of annual conference and on a greater degree of inner-party democracy the product of an obsessive constitutionalism: it was simply due to the knowledge, based upon the most extensive and consistent experience, that their leaders could not be trusted to pursue the left-wing policies which the activists wanted, and it stemmed from the hope (whether realistic or not is not here the issue) that they could force socialist virtue upon them. What the left activists wanted to avoid was a situation such as that which occurred in the sixties, under the Wilson Government, when, in Lewis Minkin's words, 'the authority of the Conference sunk to a new low as the Government carried out a range of policies dramatically opposed to Conference decisions', and when 'defeats for Government policy at Conference became as repetitive as they were ineffectual'.[28] Labour's defeat in the election of 1970, after the bitter disappointment of the previous six years, gave a new impetus to left activism; and the determination of activists to effect a change was fortified by the experience of the Labour governments from 1974 to 1979, when the promise of Labour's election manifesto of February 1974 to effect 'a fundamental and irreversible shift in the balance of power and wealth in favour of working people and their families' was never allowed to ruffle the orthodoxy of Labour's policies in office.

By the late seventies, however, the control which the Labour leaders had traditionally enjoyed over the decision-making process in the Labour Party was beginning to be seriously eroded. By far the most important element of that control, the trade-union block vote, was no longer assured. Union leaders, who had in any case found themselves at odds with Labour cabinets on trade-union reform and 'incomes policy',

---

[27] *Labour Party Annual Conference Report, 1970*, pp. 183–4. Note also the use of the same argument by Michael Foot, speaking as Leader of the party: 'Of course Party conference decisions must be respected but they cannot be regarded as absolute; that is, binding in every particular and upon every Labour MP in all circumstances.' (M. Foot, 'The Labour Party and Parliamentary Democracy', in the *Guardian*, 10 September 1981.)

[28] Minkin, *Labour Conference*, p. 291. Note also his observation that 'rarely in modern times can a parliamentary leadership have appeared as impervious to the policy preferences of its extra-parliamentary supporters as the Wilson Government did in the late 1960's' (ibid., p. 317).

also came under activist pressure in the unions and were often compelled to heed it.

The wavering of support for the leadership was also reflected in the National Executive Committee of the Party.[29] On frequent occasions, this 'custodian' of conference decisions, for so long the reliable instrument of the leadership's will and the scourge of the left, now often placed a Labour prime minister and his senior colleagues in a minority, and subjected them to embarrassing criticism. Even so, the Research Secretary of the Labour Party recalls about the period 1974–9 that 'despite all our efforts to prepare careful and detailed proposals, the status of the NEC vis-a-vis the Labour Government was, in practice, that of a mere pressure group, just one among many. The outcome of our numerous delegations, representations, statements and resolutions was thus little different from those of many other pressure groups: a few minor successes, perhaps, but little of real substance in the way of changing the direction of Government policy.'[30]

However, the defeat of the Labour Government in the election of May 1979 loosened still further the grip of the leadership on the party. Within the next two years, activists in the constituencies and in the unions, with the help of some activist organizations such as the Campaign for Labour Party Democracy, had achieved some striking successes: not only were Labour MPs now compelled to submit to a more serious process of reselection (at least where the constituency party so wished), but the Parliamentary Labour Party was also deprived of the monopoly it had enjoyed in the election of the leader and the deputy leader of the party, and was now forced to share that right with constituency parties and trade unions, in an electoral college where the Parliamentary Labour

[29] Trade unionists constitute the largest group on the NEC (twelve), followed by seven representatives of the constituency parties, elected by the constituency parties, with five women members elected by the whole conference, meaning in effect with the consent and support of the trade unions. The remainder of the Executive is made up of the Leader, the Deputy Leader, the Treasurer, a representative of the Young Socialists, and a representative of affiliated socialist societies.

[30] G. Bish, 'Working Relations between Government and Party', in K. Coates (ed.), *What Went Wrong. Explaining the Fall of the Labour Government* (1979), p. 164. At a meeting held in February 1977 between members of the Labour Government and the NEC to reconcile differences between them, 'Mr Callaghan has made it abundantly clear to the executive', *The Times* reported, 'that the Government was determined to adhere to its central economic policy and that there was no question of adopting an alternative strategy. He told the left-wing critics that they would not convince the Chancellor of the Exchequer to change his policy and he shared Mr Healey's view. "You really cannot ask us to change policy because some of you do not believe in it", Mr Callaghan said.' (*The Times*, 17 February 1977.)

Party was in a minority. The proposal to give the NEC the final say in the contents of Labour's electoral manifesto (instead of having this shared between the NEC and the cabinet or shadow cabinet) was rejected at the 1980 annual conference, and again in 1981; but it is unlikely that this issue (or any other) has thereby been finally settled.[31]

It is worth while here to note how effective the Labour Party was in isolating and 'marginalizing' one part of the British left, which might otherwise have gained greater support than it did, namely the Communist Party.

Like the trade-union leaders, and in alliance with them, the Labour Party's leaders had from the start been hostile to groupings on their left, and explicitly rejected the Marxism which some of these groupings professed. They welcomed the decision of the Marxist Social Democratic Federation, which had affiliated to the Labour Representation Committee upon the latter's foundation in 1900, to leave it in 1901; and they opposed with great energy all militant movements on their left in the years preceding the First World War. But the division between them and their opponents on the left was given an institutional and much harder form with the Bolshevik Revolution and the foundation of the Third International in 1919. From 1917 onwards, Labour leaders were among the main European opponents of Bolshevism within social democracy, and played a major role in the post-war revival of a social-democratic international trend absolutely opposed to Bolshevism; and they saw the Labour Party itself as an essential weapon in that struggle. Sidney Webb was expressing a common view when he wrote to a correspondent in November 1918 that 'the best safeguard against "Bolshevism" is a strong Labour Party in Parliament, voicing the discontent and bringing to light the grievances of the masses . . . If you *want* a Bolshevist Revolution in this country, the surest way to get it is to succeed in eliminating or discrediting the Labour Party! It is not too much to say that the survival of any popular respect for Parliamentary institutions *depends* on there continuing to be a strong and independent Parliamentary Labour Party, functioning as "H. M. Opposition".'[32]

[31] The attempt to lodge ultimate control of the electoral manifesto in the NEC was influenced by what had happened on previous occasions and notably before the election of 1979, when two years of preparatory work by the NEC and its working groups only found a dim and distorted echo in a draft manifesto prepared in the Prime Minister's office, which became the basis of hurried discussions held by a joint meeting of the Cabinet and the NEC. (Bish, 'Working Relations', p. 165.)

[32] N. Mackenzie (ed.), *The Letters of Sidney and Beatrice Webb*, iii (1978), 111. This attitude to Bolshevism did not, however, prevent the Labour leaders from

This hostility to Bolshevism was naturally directed also to the Communist Party which came into being in 1921; and it was thereafter one of the main objects of the Labour leaders to protect the Labour Party and its members from the challenge and blandishments of the Communist Party. From the beginning, their task was greatly facilitated by Communist strategies and rhetoric, and by their being able to point to the undeviating acceptance by Communists of the dictates of an increasingly Russian-dominated and then Stalinized Third International. But the essential division throughout lay in the realm of ideological commitment and political perspectives: the Communists were committed to a revolutionary transformation of British society, and to the achievement of that transformation by the waging of class struggle outside Parliament as well as inside — with much greater emphasis on the struggle outside. It was this beyond all else which made them totally unacceptable to Labour leaders committed to a purely parliamentary strategy of advance.

In June 1921 the Labour Party Annual Conference overwhelmingly endorsed the rejection by the Labour leaders of the Communist Party's application for affiliation to the Labour Party; and this was reaffirmed in 1922.[33] It was still possible for a member of the Communist Party, S. Saklatvala, to stand as a Labour Party candidate for North Battersea in the election of 1923, and to be elected. As the 1924 annual conference, however, not only was the rejection of affiliation endorsed yet again, but the conference also agreed that no member of the Communist Party would henceforth be eligible for endorsement as a Labour candidate for parliamentary or local elections; and it was also agreed that membership of the Communist Party was incompatible with membership of the Labour Party.[34] This was further tightened in 1928, to the

threatening in 1921, for the first and only time in the Labour Party's history, that 'the whole industrial power of the organized workers' would be used for what were clearly 'non-industrial' purposes, namely preventing the war against Russia towards which the British Government appeared to be moving in August of that year. (See *Labour Party Annual Conference Report, 1921*).

[33] The vote on the first occasion was 4,115,000 to 224,000 (*Labour Party Annual Conference Report, 1921*, p. 167); on the second occasion, it was 3,086,000 to 261,000 (*Labour Party Annual Conference Report, 1922*, p. 199).

[34] At the 1924 conference, the rejection of affiliation was carried by 3,185,000 votes to 193,000. The veto on Communist Party members standing for election under a Labour Party label was endorsed by 2,456,000 votes to 654,000. The incompatibility of membership was only carried by 1,804,000 votes to 1,546,000 (*Labour Party Annual Conference Report, 1924*, p. 131). The closeness of this last vote clearly suggests that many people in the Labour Party and the trade unions still found a lot of common ground with members of the Communist Party.

point where constituency Labour Parties and affiliated bodies were told to refrain from inviting on their platforms members of political parties not eligible for affiliation to the Labour Party. The Communists in any case embarked soon after, under direction from the Comintern, on ultra-sectarian policies, which led them to denounce the Labour leaders as 'social-fascists' with whom no co-operation was possible. When this was replaced in the thirties by a Communist policy of alliances against Fascism, they found the Labour leaders as adamant as ever in their opposition to collaboration with them: reference has already been made (see ch. 2) to some of the measures taken against Labour Party members who had fewer such inhibitions or none.

In the first eighteen months of the Second World War, the Communists were isolated by their opposition to what they declared to be an 'imperialist war'. With the German invasion of the Soviet Union in June 1941, their line switched to total support for the war; and admiration for the heroic struggles of what was now the Soviet ally no doubt helps to explain the great increase in Communist Party membership in the following years.[35] Much of this might in any case have evaporated at the end of the war; but the Cold War, which began as soon as the conflict with Germany ceased, generated a political atmosphere which made easier the task of continuing to isolate the Communists. Members of the Labour Party were expressly forbidden to join or have anything to do with a large number of 'proscribed' organizations, on the ground that they were Communist-controlled, as no doubt many of them were. One result of the prohibition was effectively to exclude many Labour activists from involvement in organizations seeking to oppose the colonial policies and military enterprises pursued by the Labour Government from the end of the war to its leaving office in 1951, and by Conservative governments in the fifties and beyond.

The point is of much more general application, and is also of the greatest importance. If the Labour Party had itself been the source of a vigorous intellectual and political life of a pronounced socialist character, its opposition to the Communist Party need not have entailed the drastic impairment of the effort to propagate socialist ideas in Britain, and the equally drastic curb on militant activity. Opposition to the Communist Party would have meant that one socialist tradition was in competition with another. But the political tradition which the Labour Party was concerned to foster was only socialist in the weakest possible sense, made up as it was of social reform and Fabian collectivism

[35] By 1943 membership of the Communist Party, which had been less than 18,000 in 1939, had shot up to well over 50,000.

seasoned with good sentiments.

This loose compound was not a serious socialist alternative to the ideas propagated by the Communist Party; and Labour's anti-Communism in practice therefore meant opposition to any ideas to the left of mild reform at home and traditional policies abroad. The weak ideological basis from which the Labour Party operated may help explain why it never engaged, as a party, in any really serious and sustained effort towards the dissemination of ideas. Another part of the explanation is no doubt that any such effort could not have avoided the discussion of dangerous doctrines such as Marxism, and would have involved the risk of contamination: it was better to let things be. But most important perhaps is the fact that the leaders of the Labour Party never thought of the party as a vehicle of ideas but rather as a political and electoral machine, whose first task was not to make converts to socialism, but to gain votes at elections. Nevil Johnson makes the point that 'parties do not bite deep into the political and social life of this country . . . British parties have not achieved (nor generally sought) a deep ideological penetration in society . . .'[36] This would seem to underestimate the degree to which the Conservative Party *has* sought to bite deep into the political and social life of Britain, and has succeeded in doing so. But the point does fit the Labour Party, at least in relation to 'ideological penetration'. There are areas of Britain where the Labour Party did become a state of mind and a way of life: in general, however, it has never become, and never sought to be, a vehicle for the dissemination of socialist ideas; this greatly weakened the resonance of such ideas in the political culture, and correspondingly strengthened the ideological and political hold of the conservative forces.

III

Gramsci's notion of hegemony has enjoyed great currency in recent years, and rightly so since it directs attention to a crucial aspect of class domination, namely its reliance not only on coercion, but also and normally even more on the acceptance by subordinate classes of moral and political precepts and notions which support and strengthen that domination. However, the term suffers from a great weakness, in that it conveys an impression of an accomplished and solid fact, whereas hegemony is actually a process of struggle, a permanent striving, a ceaseless endeavour to maintain control over the 'hearts and minds'

[36] N. Johnson, *In Search of the Constitution* (1977), p. 168.

of subordinate classes. The work of hegemony, so to speak, is never done. The danger always exists that subversive ideas, generated in the structure of society and its mode of production, and strengthened by particular circumstances and events, will cause serious breaches in the intellectual and moral defences of the social order, with potentially grave consequences. The danger, from a conservative standpoint, is all the greater in that there are always many people willing and eager to make themselves the carriers of subversive ideas; and in that such people, as seen from that standpoint, are able to take advantage of the freedom granted to them by a liberal and democratic regime. Hegemonic endeavours here meet counter-hegemonic ones; and must strive all the harder to ensure that ideas 'functional' to the social order continue to predominate.

The task is to defend and legitimate the social order, and this may be done either positively, by singing its virtues, or negatively, by insisting that whatever may be said against the social order, any radical alternative to it is certain to be worse and quite probably catastrophically worse. And the positive and negative can also be very nicely combined by arguing, as I noted in reference to parliamentarism, that while there might be ills in the existing system, they are perfectly remediable within its framework.

Many different institutions contribute to this task of legitimation and dissuasion; and one essential distinction between them is the extent of their *explicit* partisanship. Some institutions have no hesitation in proclaiming this task as one of their main functions: on the contrary, they are proud of it. An obvious instance is the Conservative Party, which consciously strives to serve as a major and unambiguous agency for the dissemination of conservative, legitimating, and anti-socialist ideas. And there are many other agencies — 'patriotic' associations, ideological lobbies, journals, magazines, and newspapers — which explicitly seek to serve the same purpose.

However, it is one of the most notable features of capitalist democracy that the majority of agencies which are in one way or another engaged on the same task do not have it as one of their explicit aims, are proud of their 'independence' and 'non-partisan' character, and deny having any ideological bias or preference at all; many of these same agencies proclaim their 'neutrality' and even their duty to remain 'above the battle'. Nor are such denials and assertions usually expressed with any intention to dissemble and deceive: they are made with the utmost conviction that they represent the truth of the matter. I will argue here that they do not, and that they are based on a misconception

of the meaning and nature of 'neutrality' and 'partisanship' in this context. The truth is that an enormous enterprise of indoctrination is carried out in Britain, day in day out, by a multitude of different agencies; but that the nature of this enterprise is often obscured.

One important reason why the claims can be advanced with a certain measure of plausibility and confidence is that the enterprise of indoctrination proceeds neither from a single source nor from a single doctrine or body of thought, as is the case in Soviet-type collec-tivist regimes. On the contrary, there is in a country like Britain, and in all capitalist democracies, a rich diversity of sources for the dissemi-nation of ideas, and a rich diversity of ideas as well, for which it is not difficult to find expression. Moreover, many institutions which fulfil a legitimating function are also the terrain of counter-hegemonic endeav-ours and struggles. This is true, for instance, of the educational system at all levels. On the whole, that system is an important part of a process of socialization which has strongly conformist and 'functional' con-notations. But it also offers possibilities of counter-hegemonic strivings; and these possibilities are used. The churches provide another example, and there are many others: in circumstances where a whole society is in a state of crisis, there are in fact few institutions which do not become to some degree arenas of conflict between legitimating and counter-legitimating forces.

Yet, and notwithstanding this diversity of sources and ideas, the notion that Britain is subject to a vast enterprise of indoctrination is accurate. It would only be inaccurate if the diversity betokened a rough equilibrium and balance between contending forces — more specifically if right and left were more evenly matched. But what in fact prevails is an extreme imbalance of forces. Much of the diversity occurs within a basically legitimating spectrum of thought; and what is outside that spectrum has far fewer resources at its command than the forces of legitimation. Furthermore, the latter are much more coherent and clear in purpose than the opposition to them. Intellectually and politically, the left is much more divided than the right; and one major part of the left, namely the Labour Party, has always played a very ambiguous role, at best, in regard to the intellectual and political attack on the status quo. And there has been nothing ambiguous at all in the attacks which Labour leaders have launched against the left inside as well as outside the party, with dire prophecies (of the self-fulfilling sort) of electoral disaster to come at the hands of 'decent, ordinary men and women who are not socialists' if the Labour Party were to adopt the doctrinaire, unrealistic, and pernicious policies

advocated by the left. The same ordinary men and women have also frequently been alerted by prominent ex-members of the Labour Party, from MacDonald and Snowden down to their recent Social Democrat successors, to the dangers presented by the left. Philip Snowden spoke in the General Election of 1931 of the Labour Party as 'Bolshevism run mad'. There have been innumerable variants of that theme, of greater or lesser sophistication, in the following half-century. But the burden of the message remains constant: the left is a menace. That this should be said by people in the Labour Party, or by people recently occupying positions of power in the Labour Party, is very useful to the forces of conservatism. There are very few instances of the same service being rendered to the forces of change by Conservative or ex-Conservative ministers and other leading Conservative figures. Such people rarely denounce Conservatism, or their former friends and colleagues, or Conservative activists, or the Conservative Party, with anything like the virulence and bitterness of their Labour counterparts.

Radio and television in Britain, and other means of communication, such as newspapers, are 'independent' institutions, in so far as they are not under the direct control or command of the government of the day. It would be absurd to suggest that this is of no consequence. Any degree of independence from the state and the government in the case of such institutions is something to be prized. But that independence is in practice much less substantial and much more limited than is usually claimed. Most of these institutions are in fact, though no doubt to varying degrees, agencies of conservative indoctrination.

As far as the BBC is concerned, its first General Manager, John Reith as he then was, gave classical expression to its true commitment when he wrote to the Prime Minister at the time of the General Strike in 1926 that 'assuming the BBC is for the people and that the government is for the people, it follows that the BBC must be for the government in this crisis too.'[37] In the same crisis, he also wrote in his diary, when the Government decided not to 'commandeer' the BBC, that 'they want to be able to say that they did not commandeer us, but they know that they can trust us not to be really impartial'.[38]

This, however, was not the real question then, nor has it been since. Some degree of bias may be assumed: the question is how much. Reith

[37] J. W. C. Reith, *Into The Wind* (1949), p. 108.
[38] C. Stuart (ed.), *The Reith Diaries* (1975), p. 96 (entry for 11 May 1926). It may be recalled that Reith helped Baldwin with the script of the 'Message to the Nation' during the General Strike, and with his election broadcast in 1929.

himself imposed a strong stamp of orthodoxy on the BBC not only in times of national crisis but throughout his long period of command of the Corporation; and it is symptomatic of the relatively weak position which the Labour Party occupied in British society and politics before the Second World War that, when Attlee complained after the election of 1931 that the Opposition had not been given enough time on the air, he was 'laughed out'.[39]

In this respect, the Labour Party's position greatly improved with the war and even more so with the accession of a majority Labour Government to office in 1945. But it was also then that the idea of 'balance' between the Government and the Opposition, which was now a firm requirement, came to be construed in such a way as to preserve the strong ideological and political bias which had always pervaded the BBC: the bias was now much less in favour of the Conservatives as against Labour, but much more, and in many ways more significantly, in favour of anything within a spectrum encompassed by respectable Conservatism at one end and right or centre Labour at the other.

It was after 1945 that the BBC (and many other institutions) made the very useful discovery that 'balance' was perfectly compatible with 'moderation' when an MP with a Conservative label confronted an MP with a Labour one, provided that the Labour MP belonged to the right or centre of the party, as the majority of Labour MPs always did. Nor did the fundamental agreement between the protagonists preclude fierce disputation: on the contrary, a very heated debate could quite easily be staged over many different issues, and thus be made to provide a simulacrum of genuine political controversy. From the forties onwards, the right sort of Labour MP, and speakers inclined to the Labour cause in general, helped radio and television meet the requirements of 'balance', *and* helped at the same time to keep political discussion within limits defined by the broad consensus that had been built in the years of war and that was consolidated in the years after it. This consensus was not strictly or rigidly defined; but it did nevertheless involve subscription to some basic positions. One of these was the wholehearted acceptance of the 'mixed economy', meaning in fact the acceptance as permanent of a capitalist economy. Another such basic

[39] T. Burns, *The B.B.C. Public Institution and Private World* (1977), p. 14. The author also notes that Churchill was denied the chance to broadcast on India in 1930, on which issue he fiercely opposed both Labour and Conservative policies; and that Chamberlain, as Chancellor of the Exchequer, saw to it in 1933 that there should be no Opposition reply to his broadcast on the 1933 Budget (ibid., p. 14).

position was support for NATO, the American alliance, and nuclear weapons. Perhaps most important of all was the acceptance of the view that all reasonable men and women, Labour, Tory, and whatever, could, beyond their political differences, find much common ground, and that not to do so was eccentric, really rather bad form, and a great bore to boot.

Of course, discordant opinions were heard on radio and television. But being discordant, they naturally jarred against the prevailing 'common sense', and could be dismissed as extreme, doctrinaire, and nonsensical; and, where the issues in question concerned Russia, the Cold War, the United States, and defence, as dangerous and unpatriotic as well.

It is not very surprising that, given their present mode of organization, radio and television in Britain should be sources of legitimation of the social order, and agencies for the transmission of ideas much more supportive of the status quo than inimical to it. If all that 'balance' means is that orthodox Conservative opinions should be matched by orthodox Labour ones, there need be no great problem about achieving it; and this is what radio and television have generally striven to achieve. Anything beyond this is a very different matter.

In 1936, the Report of the Ullswater Broadcasting Committee laid down the terms of the relationship between the BBC and the government in words which have remained apposite ever since: 'The position of the Corporation is one of independence in the day-to-day management of its business, and of ultimate control by His Majesty's Government;' but the Report hastened to add that 'we have no reason to suppose that, in practice, divergent views of the lines of the public interest have been held by the Corporation and by Government departments, or that the Corporation has suffered under any sense of constraint or undue interference'.[40] Allowing for some inevitable strains, difficulties, and collisions between the broadcasting authorities and the government of the day (or the Opposition), the congruence which the Ullswater Committee supposed to exist has in fact governed the relations between them from that day to the present. The reason for this is not that those in charge of broadcasting have been the helpless servants of governments, but that they have unequivocally dwelt within the spectrum of thought occupied by 'reasonable' men and women on the Conservative and Labour sides. Given this congruence, there was no reason for anything

[40] *Report of the Broadcasting Committee*, Cmd. 5091 (1936), paras. 51 and 52. The committee also stated that 'in serious or national emergencies we recognize that full governmental control would be necessary' (ibid., para. 57).

more than the normal and manageable clashes to be expected between people doing different and delicate jobs. Nor was there any good reason for the question of 'ultimate control' to arise and produce major crises.

Some remarks by Richard Hoggart on the 'filtering' of news on television are in this context worth quoting at some length. In a foreword to a study by Glasgow University's Media Group on the selection of television news, Professor Hoggart speaks of the most important 'filter' in the selection of news as being:

the cultural air we breathe, the whole ideological atmosphere of our society, which tells us that some things can be said and others had best not be said. It is that whole and almost unconscious pressure towards implicitly affirming the status quo, towards confirming 'the ordinary man' in the existing attitudes, towards discouraging refusals to conform, that atmosphere which comes off the morning radio news-and-chat programmes as much as from the whole pattern of reader-visual-background-and-words which is the context of the television news.[41]

This is well said; but it does leave out of account the quite *conscious* pressures which make for conformity. As if to rebut this criticism, Professor Hoggart goes on to reject what he calls 'low conspiracy theory' and 'high conspiracy theory'. However, one might be forgiven for thinking that he makes a better case for such theories than against them. Thus, he says that in the 'low conspiracy theory', 'it is assumed that orders are given that *this* shall be shown and *this* not, that telephone calls from high places decide what stresses there shall be and so on'. 'There *are* sometimes pressures of this kind,' he grants; 'it would be jejune to deny that they exist at all.' But 'they are neither as frequent nor as important as some romantics would like to think'.[42] Professor Hoggart may be right; but one cannot help wondering how he knows with what frequency telephone calls are made, or how important they are. Nor in any case does it take many telephone calls to create a certain atmosphere.

As for the 'high conspiracy theory', it relies, says Professor Hoggart, not on the 'direct order from Downing Street' idea, but on a 'much less direct approach', based on the idea that:

the agenda is very tightly framed, in its inclusions, omissions and stresses, not by direct orders but by a number of more hidden forces, by – first – the process of recruitment to the profession itself (so that real dissidents to the prevailing concept of 'news' don't get in or don't stay

[41] Glasgow University Media Group, *Bad News* (1976), vol. i, p. x.
[42] Ibid., p. xi.

in), by the unspoken but nevertheless firm transmission of the knowledge that *this* is how you tackle, say, questions about race, or strikes in the motor industry, or the troubles in Northern Ireland; that, where the media are so *implicitly* controlled in their agenda-setting functions, direct pressures are rarely needed.[43]

This seems very convincing; and Professor Hoggart himself says that it is 'a line which can be very usefully followed a long way'. But it does not, he adds, 'take you all the way'. For, he notes, pressure is not only applied in capitalist countries: it is far greater in Communist countries. Also, 'in commercial democracies such as Britain, the agenda is not *wholly* structured'; and there are people in broadcasting who do believe that 'the *effort* at objectivity and neutrality is important beyond all outside pressures'.[44] All such qualifications may be readily accepted; but they can hardly be said to demolish the case which Professor Hoggart makes, namely that there are powerful and effective pressures towards conformity exercised in the presentation of news and current affairs on television and radio.

One of Lord Reith's successors as Director-General of the BBC, Sir Hugh Greene, has rejected any such notion of pressure in terms which are also of interest:

The ultimate responsibility for the conduct of the affairs of the B.B.C. lies with our Governors, who are appointed by the Queen-in-Council — that is to say by the Government of the day. Once appointed they act in the interests of the B.B.C. and not in the interests of the Government or of any other political party with which they as individuals may happen to sympathise. They have been described correctly as 'trustees in the national interest'.[45]

But the notion of 'trusteeship' does not in the least preclude a strong conformist bias and an emphatic stress on the governmental and official view, on the Reithian principle noted earlier. Anthony Smith has said that 'news is an internalisation of the broadcasting organisation's or the editorial office's sense of political realities. It expresses, it almost ritualises, the organisation's own picture of the society to which it is broadcasting.'[46] But that picture is not likely to be very critical of the existing structure of power and privilege; and the broadcasting organization's 'sense of political realities' is much more likely than not to be congruent with that of the powers-that-be.

There are very infrequent occasions when the 'political class' is badly

---

[43] Ibid., p. xi. [44] Ibid., p. xii.
[45] H. Greene, *The Third Floor Front* (1969), p. 67.
[46] A. Smith, *The Shadow in the Cave* (1973), p. 98.

divided on a major issue, and when the bias towards the 'official' view is less pronounced. The Suez expedition of 1956 is an outstanding case in point. Such episodes, as well as other and frequent disagreements between the government and the broadcasting authorities, show that radio and television are not *simply* agencies of official propaganda; but this does not mean that, in addition to all else that they do, they are not *also* such agencies. As crisis and conflict grow, so must this part of their activities be expected to grow as well.

The claim that Britain has enjoyed an 'independent' and 'politically neutral' broadcasting system is only true in an exceedingly narrow and highly misleading interpretation of these words. In any larger and more accurate sense, the claim is spurious, and indeed nonsensical. For such a system is not to be had under centralized state control; and there is indeed a sense in which it is not to be had under any system. The best that can be hoped from the present system is that it should show rather less bias towards the predominant forces in society, and that it should make possible more criticism of dominant ideas and established institutions. But anything coming closer to a genuine 'balance' would, as a preliminary, require a drastic change in the balance of forces in society itself, and a labour movement sufficiently strong politically, intellectually, and organizationally, to create a broadcasting system in which it would have its own stations transmitting programmes alongside other stations representing other social and political forces and interests, and competing in a genuinely pluralistic situation, without spurious claims of 'neutrality' and 'non-partisanship'.

Unlike the BBC and commercial broadcasting, newspapers are largely free from state regulation. They do labour under a set of constraints, from the laws of libel to the Official Secrets Acts and 'D' Notices. The latter are formally intended to constrain newspapers in regard to defence matters but are also capable of being used more widely and interpreted to cover matters unrelated to defence. But leaving this aside, newspapers have none of the obligations imposed upon the broadcasting authorities. For the latter, the state is the final authority; for the press it is not. This is what is conventionally meant by 'freedom of the press'. However, this interpretation obscures the *other* constraints which affect it, and which turn most newspapers into agencies of legitimation and organs of conservative propaganda.

The first and most important of these constraints is that newspapers are part of capitalist enterprise — not only business but big business. 'In 1973,' one writer has noted, 'the three biggest conglomerates

controlled 81% of national Sunday sales and 72% of national daily sales.[47] A second important constraint is that newspapers are part of the world of business in a different sense as well, namely in the sense that they depend on the custom of advertisers.

Proprietors may or may not choose to exercise direct influence on their newspapers; and the direct influence of advertisers may not in any case be substantial. But the fact that newspapers are an intrinsic part of the world of business fosters a strong climate of orthodoxy for the people who work in them. So does the concern of editors and senior journalists to maintain good relations with governments and ministers, civil servants, and other important people in the political and administrative Establishment.

These constraints, however, do no great violence to the people actually in charge of newspapers and occupying influential positions in the journalistic hierarchy, simply because most of them, notwithstanding the unbuttoned and 'populist' style which much of the newspaper world affects, share the assumptions and outlook of the world of business and government. The overwhelming chances are that they would not have come to occupy the positions they hold if they did not. But the point need hardly be laboured: the fact is that *every* important newspaper in Britain dwells within the relatively narrow spectrum of thought to which I have already referred. Some newspapers are somewhat more critical of capitalist enterprise than others: but all of them are fervently for the 'mixed economy' and against any radical alternative to it. Some newspapers are more virulently opposed to militant trade unionism than others: but all of them are against it, and the nuances that exist between them rapidly disappear in times of acute social crisis, when they join in a chorus of denunciation and vilification. Some newspapers beat the patriotic drum more loudly, and are more ardent crusaders in the Cold War, than others: but at no time since 1945 have any of them failed to give full support to the basic contours of British foreign policy.[48] Some newspapers support the Conservatives; others support right-wing Labour, or the Liberals, or the Social Democrats — or more than one of these; or they may refuse to be identified with one party, and think of themselves as therefore 'neutral' and 'non-partisan'. But *none* of them has ever supported left-wing Labour, not to speak of anything further to the left. On the contrary, they have all made it a

[47] J. Curran, 'Capitalism and Control of the Press 1800–1975', in J. Curran, M. Gurevitch, and J. Wallacott, *Mass Communications and Society* (1977), p. 224.
[48] For much useful material on the manner in which newspapers deal with major issues, see S. Cohen and J. Young (eds.), *The Manufacture of News* (1973).

prime item of their business to denounce the alleged malevolence, mendaciousness and lack of patriotic fervour of the left; and they have been equally fierce in their attacks on anyone who has assumed a position of leadership of the left — Bevan in the fifties, Benn today. Anyone looking at the daily press in Britain must be struck by the diversity of format, style, and contents of newspapers. But in terms of important political assumptions and positions, the impression of diversity is superficial: the reality of it is an underlying uniformity of anti-socialist commitment, hardly relieved by the occasional (or even the regular) contribution of someone of a left-wing disposition — the tribute which underlying conservatism pays to superficial diversity.[49] There are few more significant proofs of the relative weakness of the labour movement in Britain and of its 'non-hegemonic' position than the nature of the press: with the exception of the Communist *Morning Star*, whose circulation is tiny, the trade unions and the labour movement have not had a paper on whose support they could rely since the *Daily Herald* changed owners in 1961.

Defenders of the press often argue that what it does is to reflect the views, attitudes, and prejudices of their readers. But in so far as the issue is the nature of the political content of newspapers, there is nothing to suggest that their readers, or many of their readers, would have no stomach for more radical views than are presented to them. The conservatism of the press is not a reflection of the alleged conservatism of working-class readers, but of the people who control its political content, and who seek to indoctrinate readers with their own conservative convictions and prejudices. The press, in this respect, is an important part of the process of legitimation, and provides a daily incantation to the virtues of the here and now, and a daily exorcism of any radical alternative to it.

The role which intellectuals have played in the battle of ideas between the forces of conservatism and the forces of change has been rather

---

[49] A good example of the way in which 'neutrality' is interpreted by editors and others has recently been provided by Mr Donald Telford, the editor of the *Observer*. In opposing the purchase of the paper by the Lonrho Company, Mr Telford 'expressed concern that the change in ownership might in the course of time lead to a change in the present neutral political stance of *The Observer*' (*The Times*, 30 June 1981). The context makes it clear that he meant by this that the *Observer* might come to be committed to the Conservative Party. 'Neutrality' here narrowly means non-commitment to any party; and the fact that the *Observer* has been consistently and quite virulently committed to opposing anything to the left of right-wing Labour is clearly not taken to mean any infringment of 'neutrality'.

more complex. A threefold division may be made here between those intellectuals who have sought to defend and strengthen the existing social order; those who have sought reforms in particular areas of economic, social, and political life; and those who have pressed for a thorough socialist transformation of society. The division is not absolute: conservative intellectuals have often advocated this or that reform; reforming intellectuals have often proclaimed their dedication to an ultimately socialist order, though located in the far distant future and not to be rushed; and intellectuals bent on wholesale socialist change have also wanted immediate reforms, and have differed greatly among themselves about how to achieve their larger and more radical goals. Moreover, intellectuals who at one time were bent on reform, and even on revolution, have often in time moved over to the conservative camp. Even so, this threefold division seems useful in identifying major and distinctive currents of thought and sentiment.

Intellectuals in Britain,[50] in the nineteenth century and to a lesser but very definite degree in the twentieth, have generally belonged to the first and second of these categories. In comparison, the third category has been significantly small, even in the twentieth century. Noel (now Lord) Annan once wrote of the 'intelligentsia' that it was 'a term which, Russian in origin, suggests the shifting, shiftless members of revolutionary or literary cliques who have cut themselves adrift from the moorings of family'. The distaste is evident and acute, and Lord Annan also drew a contrast he obviously found pleasing between *that* intelligentsia and 'the English intelligentsia, wedded to gradual reforms of accepted institutions and able to move between the world of speculation and government'.[51] Furthermore, 'the English habit of working through established institutions and modifying them to meet social needs only when such needs are proven are traits strongly exhibited by the intelligentsia of this country'.[52]

This characterization of English intellectuals is accurate. If the notion of 'intelligentsia' is taken to denote an intellectual stratum to a greater or lesser degree alienated from its society and regime, then England has not had much of an intelligentsia. Its intellectuals have for the most part been remarkably un-alienated, and the two worlds to which Lord Annan refers, of 'speculation' and government, have indeed

---

[50] 'Intellectuals' is here used in a fairly loose sense to denote the people who are mainly concerned with the formulation, articulation, and dissemination of ideas – theorists, publicists, academics, and the like.
[51] N. Annan, 'The Intellectual Aristocracy', in J. H. Plumb (ed.), *Studies in Social History* (1955), p. 244.   [52] Ibid., p. 285.

intersected at many points;[53] and it is only in rare circumstances that a substantial number of intellectuals have felt truly estranged from the world of power and politics. Over the last hundred and fifty odd years, perhaps only the 1930s properly qualify though a claim may also be entered for the sixties onwards.

In the nineteenth century, this general sense of rapport with their society and government caused intellectuals, even reforming intellectuals, to look with apprehension rather than hope on the entry of the working class on the political scene. Given their general acceptance of the social order, there was no reason why they should accord any welcome to the notion of the working class as its grave-digger: they had no wish to see its grave dug. On the contrary, intellectuals shared with the established classes of which they were a part a fear of 'the masses' and of their irruption (like latter-day barbarians) into the political process. All the leading figures in conservative and liberal thought from Coleridge to Hobhouse shared a common concern about the dangers of class conflict in a society whose lack of social solidarity must, they saw, produce such conflict; and they eagerly canvassed means whereby greater solidarity might be achieved, and whereby conflict might be contained and dissolved.

The means proposed took many different forms. Religion was of course greatly relied on, and countless sermons were delivered whose common theme was the need for the poor to endure and accept their lot, to submit and obey.[54] In 1869, T. H. Green was writing to Henry Scott Holland of the need to 'moralise masses'. He had entered Balliol in 1855, and his biographer has remarked that 'in Green's Oxford, religion was the obsessive issue that eclipsed all others'.[55] This may be a little shortsighted: it would seem more accurate to say that the issue which underlay all others was how to make Christianity the vehicle of greater social cohesion. This was also what Christian Socialism hoped to achieve.

Much hope was focused on education, or at least on a certain kind of education. Of people like Matthew Arnold, Carlyle, and George Eliot,

---

[53] The classic example is of course that of John Maynard Keynes, who moved with perfect ease between the world of Cambridge and Bloomsbury on the one hand, and the world of the state and high finance on the other. Keynes knew where he stood: 'The *Class* war' he wrote in 1925, 'will find me on the side of the educated *bourgeoisie*' ('Am I a Liberal', in *Essays in Persuasion* (1932), p. 324).

[54] See for instance J. Hart, 'Religion and Social Control in the mid-nineteenth century', in A. P. Donajgrodski (ed.), *Social Control in 19th Century Britain* (1977).

[55] M. Richter, *The Politics of Conscience. T. H. Green and his Age* (1964), p. 31.

it has been aptly remarked that 'like most of their educated contemporaries, they looked to a nation-wide system of primary education to inculcate deference in the children of the lower classes and equip them to receive instruction from their betters'.[56]

John Stuart Mill's thought embodies larger concerns; but it also exhibits the apprehensions which beset even the most advanced and progressive intellectuals at the prospect of majority rule. Mill had no wish to defend the rule of wealth and privilege. Instead, he placed his hopes in a democratic suffrage tempered and qualified by the rule of an educated élite, that would prevent 'class legislation' from whatever quarter. This impartiality masked the fact that it was the propertied classes which did rule, and that it would take a great accretion of working-class power even to begin redressing the balance; and Professor Graham Duncan is also right to note that 'the division between educated and uneducated roughly corresponded to that between rich and poor, with the result that what from one angle seemed a protection of superior merit was from another a defence of property'.[57]

With the growth of the labour movement in the second half of the nineteenth century, social reform came to occupy a central place in the arsenal of means proposed for the purpose of containing social conflict and achieving solidarity; and this was quite often advocated by intellectuals (and politicians) as an antidote to socialism, and as constituting the best defence against it. But there also occurred in the last decades of the century an important shift among a good many intellectuals from an occasional linkage with labour, over such issues as social reform and civic rights, to a much more definite and 'organic' commitment to the labour movement, and with a more comprehensive programme of economic, social, and political reform; and even in some cases, of whom William Morris is the outstanding example, to a commitment to the revolutionary transformation of society.

From the eighties onwards, a growing number of intellectuals came to 'adopt' the world of labour, and to feel themselves as in some ways part of it, even though the world of labour might not always reciprocate the feeling. What had been a trickle in the eighties became a flood in subsequent decades, and was greatly strengthened with the emergence and consolidation of the Labour Party as a major political force.

This connection of reforming intellectuals with the Labour Party and the labour movement had a strongly pedagogic impulse, with educated and competent professional people seeking to guide untutored

[56] F. B. Smith, *The Making of the Second Reform Bill* (1966), p. 241.
[57] G. Duncan, *Marx and Mill* (1973), p. 281.

trade-union leaders and others. One of the early Fabians, Graham Wallas, noted that the British labour movement did not have 'a Socialist clergy, such as the German social democrats had created, charged with the duty of thinking for the working class'.[58] Many Fabian intellectuals would no doubt have recoiled from such a crass formulation, but they would have found entirely acceptable the notion of a 'Socialist clergy' guiding the working class; and they would have seen themselves as constituting such a clergy.

However, the important issue is not simply the 'élitism' which this implies or expresses: to concentrate on this is to miss the fact that it was for the most part a certain *kind* of political guidance that was being offered – away from 'wild' strivings, unreasonable militancy, doctrinaire Marxism, and towards gradual, piecemeal, and moderate reform within the framework of the political system and in accordance with its political, parliamentary, and electoral procedures.

This is a critical aspect of the connection of the majority of intellectuals with the Labour Party and the labour movement: their predominant influence was, from the beginning, directed towards the reinforcement of the 'moderate' tendencies of the Labour leaders, and toward the supply of an intellectually and politically coherent defence and justification of these tendencies. It is no exaggeration to say that these Labour intellectuals constituted themselves into an ideological 'praetorian guard' of the Labour leaders, comparable to the trade-union 'praetorian guard' provided by union leaders.

It was natural that Labour intellectuals should want to play this role, given the un-alienated character of their relation to the social and political system, to which I referred earlier. However genuine and serious their criticisms of it might be, they remained solidly rooted in it, and sought its detailed reform rather than its wholesale reconstruction. Nor did they doubt that whatever was wanted by way of reform could be achieved within the given political framework, which was not far removed from their ideal of what a democratic system ought to be.

Left-wing intellectuals who did not accept the ideological positions of the Labour leaders and of their intellectual allies could choose one of two courses. They could work in the Labour Party and try to convert its leaders and whoever else would listen to their own views and policies.[59]

---

[58] P. Clarke, *Liberals and Social Democrats* (1978), p. 139.

[59] The most notable example of such intellectuals is Harold Laski, who had a considerable influence on Labour Party activists: he was elected to the National Executive Committee from the Constituency Section every year from 1936 until 1948. His influence on the party's leaders, on the other hand, is far from evident. For a biographical memoir, see K. Martin, *Harold Laski 1893–1950* (1953).

Alternatively, they could seek to make their influence felt in socialist groupings to the left of the Labour Party, notably the Communist Party, or as independent writers and publicists. It is very notable that very few middle-class intellectuals, until the late thirties, chose the Communist Party as a suitable agency for the advancement of their political purposes, even though Marxism had by then acquired a greater reach among intellectuals than it had previously. There existed in the twenties a lively working-class Marxist culture, nurtured and disseminated by working-class and self-taught activists, mainly in the Communist Party. Stuart Macintyre notes that 'until the sectarian barriers went up in the aftermath of 1926, Marxism was an active component in the ideology of the post-war labour movement, enabling the self-educated working class enthusiasts to reach a much wider audience through trade unions, trades councils, ad hoc organisations, and even many local Labour parties as well as the labour colleges'.[60] It was not until the thirties, under the impact of the Great Depression, the collapse of the Labour Government in 1931, Fascism, and the threat of war, that middle-class intellectuals came in any substantial numbers to be seriously interested in Marxism. But contrary to a widely held belief, Marxist thought in the thirties never came anywhere near to acquiring the hold which Fabianism had over the labour movement, and certainly over its leaders.

This 'Fabian' orientation was further reinforced in the decades following the Second World War, when new generations of Labour intellectuals engaged, like their predecessors but with even greater determination, in the task of weaning the labour movement away from radical versions of socialism, which they now proclaimed to be not only pernicious but obsolete, because of the arrival of 'post-capitalist' society. Some of the ammunition for this ideological struggle against the left was drawn from the United States, where the post-war years witnessed a great production of apologetic literature on the new capitalism. J. K. Galbraith's *American Capitalism: The Concept of Countervailing Power*, published in 1952, was an early and influential work in this vein; his *The Affluent Society*, published a few years later, was even

---

[60] Macintyre, *A Proletarian Science*, p. 97. Macintyre also notes the bitter ideological struggles that were waged between Marxists and social democrats after the First World War. One of its sites was the Workers' Educational Association, which expanded rapidly during the twenties: 'The WEA received state financial assistance, its teachers were predominantly university-trained from outside the ranks of the working class, and it explicitly repudiated any partisan approach to education. Its educational philosophy can be characterized as liberal, pluralist and it resisted any clear-cut doctrine such as Marxism.' (Ibid., p. 88).

more influential. In Britain, *The New Fabian Essays*, published in 1951, was one of the early voices of the new age; the one which made the greatest impact was C. A. R. Crosland's *The Future of Socialism*, published in 1956: its basic message was that what had commonly been understood in the labour movement to be socialism had in fact no future.

Much of the thrust of this ideological effort was concerned with foreign issues, and sought to mobilize the labour movement behind the American alliance, rearmament, and what amounted to a 'bi-partisan' foreign policy. Hugh Gaitskell combined to an unusual degree the role of Labour intellectual and leading Labour politician. In 1952, he told a journalist that 'there is only one thing we have to do in the next few years, and that is to keep the Labour Party behind the Anglo-American alliance'.[61] Much of his energy after his election to the leadership of the Labour Party in December 1955 was devoted to that end, and to educating the party into an irrevocable commitment to the 'mixed economy'.[62]

It is of course impossible to say precisely how great an impact these campaigns had on Labour activists, on the labour movement at large, and on the working class: but it is reasonable to assume that it was considerable, particularly since 'revisionist' Labour intellectuals received vociferous support from the press and other organs of opinion in their battles with the left. I noted earlier that by no means all activists were committed to the left: and many must have been swayed by men and women who were trusted members of the Labour Party and whose message was heard with attention and respect. Beyond the ranks of the activists, there was the great mass of working-class Labour voters and others: and it was a matter of the greatest importance in the shaping of their political culture that leaders of the Labour Party and of the trade unions, as well as large numbers of Labour intellectuals, should have combined to attack socialist ideas and proposals. In so far as the working class needs what Frank Parkin has called a 'radical value system', meaning a 'moral framework which promotes an *oppositional* interpretation of class inequalities', it has in Britain been rather poorly served by its own institutions in meeting that need; and it has as a result been all the more vulnerable to what Parkin also calls

[61] P. M. Williams *Hugh Gaitskell* (1979), p. 304.

[62] For some interesting material on American involvement in the debates in the labour movement on both internal and external issues, see R. Fletcher, 'Who Were *They* Travelling With?', in F. Hirsch and R. Fletcher, *The CIA and the Labour Movement* (1977).

the *'dominant* value system', meaning a 'moral framework which promotes the endorsement of existing inequality'.[63] The working class not only had to cope with the daily assault on its consciousness conducted by innumerable agencies of capitalist society whose purpose it *was* to promote acceptance of the existing social order: it also had to cope with the assault on its consciousness by people speaking from within the institutions of the labour movement, and no less insistent than their conservative counterparts about the dangers of anything to the left of 'moderate' Labour.

This combined enterprise undoubtedly had an impact and greatly reduced the appeal of socialist ideas. But the complete success of the enterprise depended on the fulfilment of certain conditions which stubbornly failed to materialize – continued economic growth and 'affluence', the elimination of crises, the maintenance of full employment, the improvement in collective services and in the 'quality of life', the reduction in class inequalities, and so on. The fact that none of this was achieved rendered the task of ideological and political containment much more difficult and problematic. Organized labour might not be very socialist; but it remained stubbornly militant in the defence of what it conceived to be its interests and traditional rights. In fact, its militancy grew in the sixties and seventies; and so did its willingness to listen to activists in its own ranks. For all the brave assurances of imminent social pacification in a post-capitalist society freed at last from ideological division and class conflict, there was in fact great division and conflict, which political parties were less able to contain and control than in the past. This meant that the state was more than ever required to intervene in the containment of pressure and the management of conflict. The state plays a unique and indispensable role in this respect; and it is with the ways in which it has played this role in Britain that the next chapter is concerned.

[63] F. Parkin, *Class Inequality and Political Order* (1977), p. 82.

4. *THE MANAGEMENT OF CLASS CONFLICT*

I

Different parts of the state each make their own particular contribution to the management of class conflict; but before this contribution is discussed, some preliminary considerations of a general character about the state and government are in order.

It is of course elementary that a distinction must be made between the state and government — the latter is only one part of the former. But the distinction has a particular meaning and importance in capitalist democracy, and even more particularly in its British version. This is that the government is directly subject to a large variety of political pressures from competing and conflicting forces in society, while the rest of the state system (with the exception of local government) is not. This is in no way to imply that the other parts of the state system — the civil service, the judiciary, the military and police apparatus, etc. — are not 'political', and do not fulfil a 'political' role: the functions they perform have a direct bearing on the maintenance and defence of the existing social order and therefore necessarily do have strong 'political' connotations. The point is rather that these other parts of the state system are largely or even wholly immune from direct political pressures, notably from below, while governments in a capitalist democracy are subject to them and have to manage them.

Of the pressures to which governments are subjected, the most important by far have been those of capital on the one hand, and those of labour on the other. Their demands are antagonistic and produce conflict: the task of the state has been to ensure that the requirements of capital (which does not mean its every demand) are met, but not so as to create conditions of dangerously explosive alienation of the working class.

I have already argued earlier that the pressures which capital is able to exercise upon government and the influence which it wields are very much greater than those of labour; and this requires further discussion. One aspect of this preponderance of capital is that *all* governments in Britain have consistently been the conscious allies of capitalist enterprise, and have wanted to help and defend it. This was true for Whig and Tory governments in the nineteenth century and it has remained so for Labour as well as Conservative ones in the

twentieth. The ways in which Labour governments have wanted to help and defend capitalist enterprise have not always been to the latter's taste; and even Conservative governments have often been found wanting by one part or other of capital. This points to an important aspect of the character of the state – its 'relative autonomy' – which will be considered presently. But the state's purpose has always been unambiguous, namely to help capitalist enterprise to prosper. Nor is this surprising, given the belief, shared by all Conservative ministers and most Labour ones, that the health and success of capitalist enterprise are synonymous with the 'national interest'. Labour governments might also want to see a public sector prosper alongside the private one; but they have always viewed such a public sector as subsidiary to the private one, and even as subordinate to it; and this has always been even more strongly the view of Conservative governments. The 'mixed economy' has always meant a mix which gave to capitalist enterprise an overwhelmingly predominant place in economic life, with the public sector intended to serve the private one by providing 'infra-structural' services to it. The alternative perspective, which was to embark on the task of creating an economy in which it was the public sector which occupied a preponderant place in the 'mixed economy', has never commended itself to any Labour government, even though the achievement of the 'common ownership of the means of production, distribution and exchange' has been one of the Labour Party's 'objects', formally inscribed in its constitution, for well over half a century. In fact, the opposition of Labour leaders to anything more than marginal public ownership has been one of the main grounds of contention between them and left-wing activists wanting to go much further.

The commitment which both Labour and Conservative governments have had to capitalist enterprise is clearly a matter of paramount importance in regard to state policy: for it places the nature of the economic order beyond serious questioning; and it also means that most other questions of policy come to have capitalist enterprise as a crucial point of reference, since it is of such great importance in the whole life of society.

This points to the main reason, already noted in Chapter 3, for the predominant position of capital, namely the power which it actually wields, by virtue of its control of the larger part of the country's industrial, commercial, and financial means of activity, and its capacity to make decisions of vital concern not only to the particular firm but to many interests beyond it, up to the whole of society. Capital presents an image of itself as curbed, cribbed, and confined by uncaring

politicians and interfering bureaucrats. In reality, governments find it extremely difficult to exercise effective control over private economic activity, except in time of war. Conservative governments have not wanted to exercise such control anyway; and such attempts as Labour governments have made since 1945 to achieve control and to 'plan' the economy have never, in concrete terms, amounted to very much. Stuart Holland quotes a document issued in 1949 by the Department of Economic Affairs (established by the Labour Government in 1964 and now defunct) which succinctly stated that 'what happens in industry is not under the control of government'.[1] This may serve as an appropriate epitaph for all experiments in 'planning' undertaken by Labour governments since 1945.

No doubt, more resolute governments might have achieved more. But the issue is not simply one of will and determination: there are very large political and administrative problems which confront any government seeking to control a predominantly private economy.

Nor are these pressures and problems only generated at home: at least as important are the international ones. Throughout the post-war years, and until sterling became a 'petro-currency', governments were exceedingly vulnerable to financial and other pressures from abroad; and their vulnerability has only been very partially mitigated by North Sea oil. Labour governments in particular found that the price of the loans and credits they wanted from abroad was detailed surveillance of their economic and social policies. International pressures were combined with domestic ones, and greatly reinforced them. In their opposition to government policies, capitalist interests (and their allies in the state system) found precious support from foreign sources. As Fred Hirsch noted in 1977, 'the IMF is largely the vehicle by which domestic groups, including City, Banks, and Treasury, can get extra power behind their elbows to jog Her Majesty's elected Ministers'.[2]

Conservative governments have always had less of a problem in this respect than Labour ones, because of the basic confidence which they inspire in the right quarters, whatever differences there may be over specific policies; and such governments are indeed unlikely to stray far off the path of economic orthodoxy. Labour governments, for their part, and despite their 'moderation', confront much greater difficulties, with interests who view them, their policies, and their purposes, with great suspicion or downright hostility, and for whom a Labour

---

[1] S Holland, *The Socialist Challenge* (1975), p. 25.
[2] The *Guardian*, 18 January 1977. Hirsch was himself a former IMF official, who subsequently became Professor of International Studies at Warwick University.

government, of whatever kind, seems an offence against nature. The difficulties this presents need not be thought insurmountable: but they are clearly formidable. It is a common view that the power of the state is very great and growing; and this is in many ways true. But in relation to the actual control which it has over capitalist enterprise, it is rather its relative weakness which is remarkable. This is well appreciated in regard to international firms, whose freedom from effective constraint by national governments is considerable; but for different reasons and to a lesser extent, it applies internally as well.

However, this does not mean that capital is able to get the state to do all it wants, and never to do what it does not want: other and conflicting influences affect the state's policies and actions. Business must therefore exert itself as a pressure group; and its power and resources, as well as the sympathetic view which governments and officials generally take of its activities, make it in fact by far the strongest pressure group in the land. It has a pre-eminent place in the councils of the Conservative Party, whose financial well-being largely depends on contributions from the world of business. It can count on the unswerving support of many Members of Parliament, of whom a considerable number are themselves part of that world; and large numbers of MPs can be relied on to be the vigorous and vigilant champions of capitalist enterprise, in the House of Commons and in the country. Nor is the House of Lords wanting in this respect: many of its active members are well entrenched in the upper reaches of capitalist enterprise, industrial, financial, and commercial. As was noted in the last chapter, business can be assured of the goodwill and support of a virtually unanimous press: in any encounter between business and a Labour government (or a Conservative one for that matter), it is usually the government which will come off worst in the newspapers. The press will occasionally criticize, in sorrow rather than in anger, some business misdemeanour or dereliction, and condemn what Edward Heath once called, in respect of one company, the 'unacceptable face of capitalism'. But these are exceptions to the dominant attitude of newspapers, which is that the present economic system, whatever specific faults may be ascribed to it, is immeasurably the best that is to be had in a necessarily imperfect world.

Nevertheless, the government and the state do not and cannot, least of all in a capitalist democracy, act as the mere 'instrument' of capital. No government, in conditions of universal suffrage and political competition, can altogether ignore other forces, with different and often contradictory interests. The most important of these forces, in general

terms, is organized labour. Trade unions, for all the limitations and constraints on their power, are pressure groups which governments have to reckon with, and the goodwill of whose leaders they have traditionally sought to retain, even in periods of 'confrontation'.[3] Indeed, it is often in such periods, or shortly after the crisis has passed, that governments make some concessions at least to union demands, even though business is opposed to concessions being made.

Beyond organized labour, there stands the rest of the working class, as an electoral force. General elections are a constraining point of reference for governments. Prime ministers and their colleagues may not allow themselves to be greatly worried by the thought of a general election in the early years of a government's life, and may feel that they can safely disregard unfavourable opinion polls, or by-election defeats, or local election losses. But as time goes on and a general election looms nearer, a government is likely to take it more and more into account, and will seek to shape its policies so as to minimize the risk of defeat at the polls. This means the adoption of measures which, it is hoped, will have a popular appeal, whatever business may think about them.

Quite apart from elections, governments also naturally wish to avoid eruptions of popular feeling outside the channels traditionally traced out for their expression. This has always been a major concern of British governments. In these terms, the street riots which broke out in a number of English cities in July 1981 must be taken to constitute a failure for the government of the day. The causes of the riots long antedated the Thatcher Government's election in May 1979. But that Government's policies may legitimately be thought to have exacerbated the problems which caused the riots, or at least to have contributed nothing towards their alleviation. But however this may be, riots and other civil commotions constitute a negative verdict on the government under which they occur. Previous Conservative governments in the

[3] Thus Tony Lane notes that 'even in the years immediately before and after the First World War when fears of working-class revolution were at their height and force most resorted to, governments trod remarkably softly'; and this is exemplified by 'the appointment of working class magistrates, the appointment of trade unionists to the Factory Inspectorate, the Factory and Workshops Act of 1891, the Arbitration Act of 1896, the Workmen's Compensation Act of 1897, the reversal of the Taff Vale decision by the Trades Disputes Act of 1906, an Act limiting the hours of work for adult miners in 1908, the establishment of Trade Boards in 1909 to regulate wages in certain sweated industries, the beginning of state social insurance in 1911, the payment of MPs from the same year, and the legalisation of trade union political action in 1913' (T. Lane, *The Union Makes Us Strong* (1974), p. 93).

twentieth century (and earlier) have tried to prevent the occurrence of such upheavals, and have often been spurred to making concessions in order that they should not arise or recur.

What this means, generally speaking, is that governments in capitalist democracies are vulnerable to pressure from below; and this vulnerability is greatly increased by one crucial consideration for people who occupy ministerial office, namely the fact that they very much want to continue doing so. Political office-holders, in other words, have *their own interest* in mind when they weigh up policy choices; and it is not cynicism but common sense which suggests that this is uppermost in their minds, the more so since they find it easy to think that their continuation in office, and keeping their competitors out of office, is beneficial and even indispensable to the 'national interest'. But if their interest is to be served, political office-holders cannot appear to be simply the agents of business or the obedient executants of the policies favoured by capital. They must appeal to a wider constituency, appear 'reasonable', 'fair', 'even-handed': this requires much greater flexibility than would be possessed by a mere 'instrument'. To the degree that the politics of the market-place has any meaning, as it obviously has in a capitalist democracy, so must some of the promptings of the market-place be taken into account by governments.

This larger concern of political office-holders does not, in itself, present any threat to the long-term interests of capital, or of conservative forces in general: it is on the contrary essential to their preservation. If governments are to defend these interests effectively, they simply must have a considerable degree of autonomy in deciding how this is to be done, what concessions must be made to other and conflicting interests and forces, and by what means pressure from below may best be contained. This autonomy is indeed 'relative'; but it is nevertheless real. Governments are inserted in a structure of power in which capital plays a major part. But all that governments do, or fail to do, is not determined by the imperative requirements of capital or by the imperative commands of capitalists. Governments always have a lot more room than this.

This is precisely why there is a constant danger, from the point of view of conservative forces, that governments in a capitalist democracy will be tempted to make undue concessions to popular demands, and use the room they do have to court popularity to the detriment of the policies which conservative forces favour, and that they will show weakness in the face of pressure from below. The danger, from the same point of view, is particularly acute when a general election brings

a Labour government to office.

This is where the distinction between government and the rest of the state system is particularly relevant. For the other parts of the state, which are not subject to electoral fortunes and misfortunes, and which are generally much less vulnerable to popular pressures, or not vulnerable to them at all, are therefore able to act as bulwarks of continuity, stability, 'sound' and 'reasonable' policies, if need be against vulnerable and weak governments; or they can at least limit the damage which governments may cause. Universal suffrage brings a government to office: the rest of the state system sees to it that the consequences are not so drastic as to affect conservative continuity. Governments, in this perspective, are also inserted in a structure of political and administrative power *inside the state*; and the parts of that structure other than the government are of critical importance in the shaping of policy and in the determination of state action.

II

The role of top civil servants in restraining governments is obviously crucial, since it is they, in the state system, who are closest to ministers and to government in regard to the making of policy. The conventional, Establishment view of that role is well caught in a reply by Clement Attlee to a question put to him some time after his retirement by Francis Williams. 'In earlier days,' said Williams, 'many people used to suggest that a Labour Government with a socialist programme would run into trouble with right-wing civil servants. Did you have any of that difficulty?'. Attlee replied as follows:

Never. I always found them perfectly loyal. So did all the others so far as I know. I never had complaints. That's the civil service tradition, a great tradition. They carry out the policy of any given government. If they think it's silly, of course they'll tell the minister so. If he decides to go ahead, then they carry it out. There may have been some whose advice to ministers was coloured by their own personal attitudes. I never encountered them. They were all anxious to do the best they could by a Labour government.[4]

The notion that the programme of the Attlee Government was sufficiently 'socialist' to confront top civil servants with a problem need not be taken seriously. Civil servants in Britain have never had to confront

[4] F. Williams, 'A Prime Minister Remembers: The War and Post-War Memories of the Rt. Hon. Earl Attlee', in A. King (ed.), *The British Prime Minister* (1969), p. 79.

a government with a 'socialist programme'; or at least, they have never had to confront a government determined to carry out such a programme. No Labour government has ever given its civil service advisers cause to contemplate any really serious and sustained form of administrative and political resistance or to seek in earnest the defeat of its plans and policies. This tells us nothing as to what might happen in the future, or about the actual past and present role of senior civil servants. Top civil servants are generally people with conventional views, which means that, like other powerful people in Britain, they dwell, in ideological and political terms, in the spectrum of thought to which I have referred in previous pages, and which is bounded by 'moderate' Labour at one end and reactionary (but constitutional) Conservatism at the other. It is also probable that most of them would be found somewhere at the centre of the spectrum, slightly to the left or right depending on the general political climate.

This at least would seem to have been the case since the Second World War. In the inter-war years, and reflecting the weakness of Labour and the preponderance of a harsher strain of Conservatism, top civil servants were much more firmly situated at the reactionary end of the spectrum; and it may be that the notion of a spectrum is not particularly apposite for that period. Arthur Marwick has noted that 'the fundamental administrative morality of the thirties was the morality of the Means Test';[5] and it might also be said that the fundamental political morality of the inter-war years in foreign affairs was anti-Communism and, relatedly, the appeasement in the thirties of the Fascist dictators. Anti-Communism and opposition to anything to the left of 'moderate' Labour remained an essential part of respectable thinking after the Second World War (and was indeed an essential defining element of respectability, for civil servants and for everybody else in a position of power); but a much more positive view of state intervention in economic and social life also became perfectly acceptable. From being a taboo figure in official circles, Keynes became a hallowed one – until the new discredit that was attached to his name with the coming to office of the Thatcher Government. Even in the Foreign Office, long associated with strong right-wing sentiments, new winds seemed to blow as a consequence of war. At least, strong conservatism was no longer the only tenable position: moderate social-democratic positions were also permitted. 'Most Labour MPs', two Conservative ones have noted, 'continue to harbour preconceptions of diplomats as

<hr>

[5] A. Marwick, 'British Society and the Second World War', in C. Cook and A. Sked (eds.), *Crisis and Controversy* (1976), p. 160.

toffee-nosed Tories in old Etonian ties. Then, on appointment to the F.O., they suddenly find themselves surrounded by bright and deferential young men who sometimes even turn out to have voted Labour. They are swept off their feet.'[6]

Given the seismic changes brought about by the war, it was to be expected that senior civil servants should have found it very easy to work with those who led the Labour Government of 1945. They knew and had worked during the war with Attlee, Morrison, Bevin, Cripps, and Dalton, and had no fear that these men might be 'unsound', a notion which had itself undergone great changes in the war years. Nor was there much reason for any great problem to arise with the members of the Labour governments of 1964 to 1970, and from 1974 to 1979. Clashes occurred and battles were fought, as recorded in detail by Crossman, Wilson, Castle, and others; but while some of these had a certain ideological reach, it would be ridiculous to think of them as involving a socialist or radical administration desperately locked in battle with reactionary civil servants. Not all civil servants by any means were reactionary; and very few ministers were radical or socialist.

The fact that senior civil servants hold conventional views, which are part of the predominant 'common sense' of people in power, helps them to bring to their work the 'non-partisan' attitude which is thought appropriate to it. This in effect means two things. One of them is that, so far as they are concerned, it matters very little if at all that a particular policy is labelled Conservative or Labour, provided it is squarely within the framework of accepted ideas. Secondly, it means that the approved professional attitude is one of relative detachment towards any policy within that framework. Samuel Brittan wrote in 1971 of the 'air of civilized scepticism' which was to be found in many parts of Whitehall; and he went on to say that 'it is still regarded as inappropriate to show excessive enthusiasm for a new idea; and the words "There is nothing new under the sun" seem to be written on the wall in invisible ink . . . British official scepticism is more often directed towards new reforming ideas than towards accepted beliefs and is not necessarily a prelude to anything at all.'[7] This seems right; and the scepticism towards new ideas of which Brittan speaks can of course quite easily turn into strong opposition. Scepticism of this sort is a version of conservatism and of the defence of the status quo: such defence not only admits of cautious and moderate reform, but often requires it.

It would not be reasonable to expect senior civil servants to have

⁶ J. Bruce-Gardyne and N. Lawson, *The Power Game* (1976), p. 166.
⁷ S. Brittan, *Steering the Economy* (1971), p. 44.

more 'advanced' views than this. The majority of them are the products of middle- and upper-class homes, with a public-school and Oxford or Cambridge education. Such a background does not automatically and inevitably produce conformity; but it mainly does. Even those senior civil servants who do not have this background are 'socialized' into conformity by their careers in the civil service, and would not get very far if they did not give adequate proof early on that they would acquire if they did not have already the right kind of ideas and attitudes. 'Annual reports and promotions', it has recently been noted, 'are entirely in the hands of senior civil servants. They have infinitely more impact on a subordinate's career than the extremely rare ministerial "interventions".[8] This has larger implications which will be discussed presently; but it clearly places a high premium on conformity and acceptance, and is another instance of the ways in which the system keeps out potentially troublesome people. In the case of the civil service, however, the keeping-out process is supplemented and reinforced by the vetting procedures which were introduced by the Labour Government in the post-war years. It was officially said that these procedures were intended to 'weed out' Communists and Fascists from 'sensitive' posts. But there was no problem with 'Fascists', and the reference to them was simply intended to suggest even-handedness of treatment for all 'extremes'. This has been found useful ever since. In fact, there was a considerable asymetry in the treatment of people on the right and on the left. For it was always acceptable for a senior civil servant to be extremely reactionary, provided he was not actually a declared Fascist, and there was not much likelihood of that; but it was not at all acceptable for a senior civil servant to be strongly left-wing, even though he was not a Communist and might even be anti-Communist. Neither the vetting procedures nor the ideological climate in the upper reaches of the civil service required a man or woman to abjure strongly held conservative views; but there was a problem for anyone with more than mildly reform-oriented leanings. A strongly critical view of the existing social order, from a right-wing perspective, was still part of the mainstream; a strongly critical view of it, from the perspective of the left, was not. People holding such views could not expect a glittering career in the civil service.

These pressures have an obvious bearing on the relation of civil servants to business. Conformity here means the acceptance of the view that capitalist enterprise, in the framework of the 'mixed economy',

[8] P. Kellner and Lord Crowther-Hunt, *The Civil Servants. An Inquiry into Britain's Ruling Class* (1980), p. 228.

must not be subjected to undue state 'interference', and that what is good for it cannot, generally speaking, be bad for the country. The state must of course intervene, but to sustain the private sector, not to hinder it or to substitute itself for it, unless this is absolutely unavoidable. Such sentiments, it should be added, are in any case fostered by the close relationship which senior civil servants have with people in the world of business, professionally and also socially; and sympathy for business rather than a critical attitude to it is likely to be further strengthened by the expectation which many senior civil servants have of entering the world of business (of course at board-room level) upon retirement.[9] No such close and sympathetic relationship exists between them and the world of organized labour; in so far as the 'rationality' of capitalism is also that of state administrators, they are much more likely to take an adverse view of the demands of trade unions, since these cut across the requirements of business, and are therefore easily taken to be contrary to the public interest which it is the task of civil servants to defend.

The ideological and political dispositions of senior civil servants would be of much less consequence if they did not wield great power in the making of policy. But they do. The picture of 'bureaucrats' running the country and of ministers as the mere executants of the wishes of their senior 'advisers' is obviously overdrawn. But the picture of civil servants as merely deferential and submissive administrators is even more inaccurate. Senior civil servants in Britain constitute a formidable bloc of power, more cohesive and resourceful than any other element in the state, with the possible exception of the cabinet, but only if the cabinet is united, and determined to have its way.

Civil servants have to deal with the politicians whom universal suffrage, party politics, and prime ministerial calculations and convenience have thrust upon them. Such reasons for ministers being in charge of departments are not likely to induce much of a sense of awe in civil servants. Everything in their education and professional experience leads them to see themselves as the guardians of the 'public interest', if need be against politicians in search of votes. Professional

[9] In relation to this, Kellner and Crowther-Hunt quote a 'disenchanted' Labour minister as follows: 'Twenty years ago it was the exception for retiring civil servants to go to jobs in industry or finance. Now it is almost the exception not to. It is not so much specific corruption as atmospheric pollution. People trim their sails expecting jobs. They are sometimes useful to their employers, knowing their way around Whitehall. I don't mind that. It's the way they drink together, play golf, or go shooting beforehand. Nothing is ever said directly; but the civil servants know what to expect.' (Ibid., p. 199.)

administrators have a strong propensity to despise democratic pressures; and a strong vein of supercilious paternalism runs through this as through any other sheltered bureaucracy. The people concerned are deeply conscious of the great complexity of the enterprise of government, and believe that it must be conducted with a measure of deliberation and detachment as well as knowledge which is, they think, very difficult if not impossible for most democratic politicians to achieve. Their opinion of such politicians is consequently not very high.[10]

Yet, politicians themselves, when they reach ministerial office, are also quite keen to fend off democratic and activist pressures, and do so on grounds not unlike those of their civil servants. The latter consider it one of their main tasks to shield ministers from these pressures; and ministers wish to be shielded without seeming heedless of democratic forms and procedures. Given this common purpose, ministers and their senior advisers find it easy to engage in a co-operative task of reducing the impact of the democratic demands made upon them by the political system. In no realm has this been more marked than in the permanent struggle against political and industrial left-wing activists: here, Conservative and Labour ministers on the one hand, and their civil servants on the other, have worked in a spirit of great harmony to neutralize and defeat what was agreed to be the enemy. But there are many other issues where the same spirit of co-operation has prevailed.

One manifestation of this ministerial and bureaucratic suspicion of democratic pressure and prying is the passion for secrecy which pervades Whitehall, and which turns large parts of government into a closed book, not to be prised open on pain of severe penalties, under the Official Secrets Acts and other constraints.[11]

Much of this passion for secrecy is based on the belief that there is much about the operation of government which it would not be 'helpful' to divulge, certainly to the general public, and also to Members of Parliament, and even, in regard to certain issues, to members of the government itself, up to and including cabinet ministers. Clement Attlee

[10] The editor of the diaries of Sir Alexander Cadogan, Permanent Under-Secretary of State for Foreign Affairs from 1938 to 1946, notes that Cadogan felt 'for many politicians an emotion bordering on contempt'. The language in which he expressed this may be unusual, but the sentiments are not: 'Silly bladders! Self-advertising, irresponsible nincompoops. How I *hate* Members of Parliament. They embody everything that my training has taught me to eschew — ambition, prejudice, dishonesty, self-seeking, light-hearted irresponsibility, black-hearted mendacity.' (D. Dilks, *The Diaries of Sir Alexander Cadogan. 1938–1945* (1971), p. 18.)
[11] For a recent example, see C. Aubrey, *Who's Watching You?: Britain's Security Services and the Official Secrets Act* (1981).

did not consult the full cabinet in 1947 on whether a British atomic bomb should be built, and this set a pattern on matters of nuclear armaments which has endured until the present.[12] The excuse is always 'security'; very often, this is a convenient escape from the constraints of democratic control and pressure.

Occasions arise when ministers, in the eyes of their senior advisers, cease to be 'reasonable' and 'co-operative', and commit themselves, for one political reason or other, to enterprises and policies which these advisers believe to be gravely mistaken and misconceived. This may well occur with Conservative ministers as well as Labour ones, but it is more likely with the latter, since Labour has traditionally been the party of reform and intervention, often in ways which have not conformed to departmental thinking. What must then be done is to steer ministers away from unsound proposals. Where such proposals cannot be altogether squashed, their most obnoxious features must be removed or attenuated. One way and another, a great deal can be done with *any* proposal, provided the will and the power are there.

Senior civil servants do have the will and the power; and they can therefore make reasonably sure that their subordination to ministers — which is one of the basic principles according to which the constitutional and political system is deemed to operate — is mostly formal, and that the relationship is one of collaboration between colleagues. Ministers do 'have the last word', but they are dependent on their civil servants for expert advice and information on matters about which they often know little or nothing, and to which they may not in any case have the time to give adequate attention before a case has to be presented or a decision made. A minister cannot hope to do really well — and ministers naturally do very much want to do well — unless he or she has the support and co-operation of the department. But there are degrees of support and co-operation, and support of the wholehearted sort is the more likely to be given, the more closely the minister's policies approximate to what the department itself thinks right and proper. Policies of which the department approves will be fought for and advanced through the Whitehall maze with all the energy and ingenuity required. Policies of which the department does not approve will have a harder time and encounter obstacles of many different kinds which the minister will find it difficult or impossible to negotiate.

---

[12] 'The decision to spend £5 billion on the Trident nuclear missile was not taken by the full Cabinet and several senior Ministers have now confirmed that their approval for the project was not sought before the announcement was made three weeks ago.' (The *Guardian*, 6 August 1980.)

A minister who has the full backing of the prime minister and the most influential members of the cabinet may be able to overcome the opposition of officials, and even enlist their co-operation. But it is precisely those ministers with radical projects and ideas who are the most likely not only to alienate their officials, but also to be seen by the prime minister as people who make life difficult. It may not be possible to dismiss them; but it is usually possible to transfer them to less 'controversial' ministries.[13] They may be excluded from key cabinet committees, where crucial decisions, which cannot be reversed in the cabinet itself, are made. Nor is it easy for radical ministers in a conventionally-minded cabinet to make a strong impact. They are surrounded by hostile and senior colleagues; and the prime minister can do a great deal to prevent awkward matters from getting much of an airing in cabinet, or even from being raised at all.[14] In short, radical ministers in an orthodox administration are vulnerable; and their vulnerability can be increased and exploited by officials in the struggle over policy.

Ministerial office in Britain isolates its holder, and leaves ministers, with all their uncertainties, to face virtually on their own a normally cohesive and experienced group of civil servants. This is a good recipe for responsibility without real power; and the introduction of 'special advisers' in departments could not be expected to redress the balance between ministers and officials. Senior civil servants have all the resources they need to neutralize and absorb such intruders, and to ensure that they do not threaten the control which permanent officials exercise.[15] Brian Chapman wrote in 1969 that 'the British civil service at the higher levels is a closed corporation of a kind unknown in most European countries'.[16] It would take a lot more than 'special advisers' or any similar device to break open that closed corporation.

[13] A recent example is that of Tony Benn, who was appointed Secretary of State for the Department of Industry by Harold Wilson when the Labour Government was formed in February 1974. Benn soon showed that he saw his task in strongly interventionist ways. This produced much opposition, not least in the cabinet itself, and Benn was transferred to the Department of Energy in June 1975.

[14] 'It is regarded as quite improper for a minister to raise any matter which has not previously been accepted for the agenda by the Prime Minister' (J. P. MacIntosh, *The British Cabinet* (3rd edn., 1977), p. 449).

[15] As a small but significant instance of this control, note that 'from the 1930s to 1970s, not only was the PM's private office dominated by the Civil Service, but it regularly drew its leading members from two departments, the Treasury and the Foreign Office' (G. W. Jones, 'The Prime Ministers' Secretaries: Politicians or Administrators', in J. A. G. Griffith (ed.), *From Policy to Administration* (1976), p. 31).

[16] B. Chapman, *British Government Observed* (1969), p. 23.

In the Godkin Lectures which he delivered at Harvard in 1971, R.H.S. Crossman argued that radical change was nevertheless possible by dint of great effort, and that civil servants would accept change if ministers pushed hard enough: 'I said,' he added, '"accept change" — of course, they often fight it. Of course they do, but that's part of their job.'[17] Whether it should be 'part of their job' is not here the issue. More to the point is that senior civil servants themselves consider it to be such, and that there is at the heart of British government a very powerful braking mechanism against radical change. Nor is that mechanism operated only by senior civil servants in departments of state. There are other people, located in official institutions, who wield great power to much the same conservative purpose. One such person is the Governor of the Bank of England, who has traditionally played a major role in helping to shape the financial and therefore the economic and social policies of governments. This has remained the case, notwithstanding the 'nationalization' of the Bank in 1946. The Governor speaks to governments with all the authority conferred upon him by the fact that he stands for financial and economic policies backed by a formidable concentration of financial power at home and abroad: what he says and does goes a very long way.

In his *apologia* for his tenure of office between 1964 and 1970, Harold Wilson recalls that the Labour Government elected in October 1964 was immediately faced with a sterling crisis, and that the Governor of the Bank of England, Lord Cromer, asked for 'all-round cuts in expenditure, regardless of social or even economic priorities, and fundamental changes in some of the Chancellor's economic announcements'. Wilson notes that he replied as follows:

Not for the first time, I said that we had now reached the situation where a newly-elected Government with a mandate from the people was being told, not so much by the Governor of the Bank of England but by international speculators, that the policies on which we fought the election could not be implemented; that the Government was to be forced into the adoption of Tory policies to which it was fundamentally opposed.

The Governor, according to Wilson, 'confirmed that this was, in fact, the case', and that this was due to 'the sheer compulsion of the economic dictation of those who exercised decisive economic power'. Wilson in turn said that he was not willing to accept this, that the Governor's arguments meant that 'not only were social progress and indeed the

[17] R. H. S. Crossman, *Inside View* (1972), p. 77.

whole of our mandate for reform in danger; so was democracy itself': 'To accept his argument would mean that the Queen's First Minister was being asked to ring down the curtain on parliamentary democracy, by accepting the doctrine that an election in Britain was a farce, that the British people could not make a choice between policies, and that the policies were directed from outside the country . . .'[18] This account would be a lot more edifying if the Wilson Government had not in fact pursued throughout its period of office economic and social policies (not to speak of foreign ones) orthodox enough to be broadly acceptable to 'those who exercised decisive economic power'. This has been the case under successive governments of both parties, and it explains why it has been possible for top administrators to co-operate with whatever government came to office: there was no occasion for any major crisis. The point will be met again in relation to other parts of the state.

III

It is a fundamental principle of the British constitutional and political system that the military and the police are subordinate to the government of the day, whatever its political complexion may be. Broadly speaking, this has in fact been so. Police and military chiefs have had a certain degree of autonomy in their own domains; and they have contributed to the making of policy in regard to matters of special concern to them. There have also been occasions when they have been at odds with the government; and military chiefs have always constituted a formidable lobby on behalf of the armed services, and over issues of defence and strategy. But it is only very rarely that this has caused a really major problem for the government of the day. Much more commonly, the military and the police have found no great difficulty in serving their political superiors. The main reason for this is the same as in the case of top civil servants, namely that the purposes which governments have sought to serve have not been fundamentally different from those of the police and military branches of the state. No doubt, Labour governments — and even more so individual Labour ministers — have aroused suspicion and hostility on the part of conservative-minded policemen and military men; but no so as to make collaboration impossible or unduly difficult.

This broad congruence has made it possible for both police and

[18] H. Wilson, *The Labour Government. 1964-1970* (1971), pp. 37-8.

military chiefs to maintain a 'low profile' in political terms. They are required to avoid any political identification, or the public display of any party bias; and the image that has traditionally been powerfully fostered is that the police and the armed forces are politically neutral, and solely concerned with serving the state, society, and the 'public interest'.

As already noted, however, these are not 'neutral' activities; and it is in fact much more realistic to see the police and the military as a crucial element in the containment of pressure from below. It is of course possible to think of this as serving the state, society, and the public interest; but it is also possible to think of it as the service of a system of class inequality and domination, and as thus having profoundly 'political' connotations.

The police is a containing and coercive agency; and the military has or may also be given police functions. These functions involve much more than the containment and coercion of pressure from below: but this is nevertheless of pre-eminent importance. Where there is a strike, there are also the police, and occasionally the military, as regulating and possibly repressive forces, and in the case of the military, as a strike-breaking agency where so required by the government. Strikers and pickets may be 'handled' in different ways, ranging from relative tolerance to gross brutality: but there is never any doubt that strikers and pickets are on one side, the police (and the military) on the other. The same is true of the political demonstrations, marches, meetings, and other such activities in which the left is engaged. The police also acts as a constraining influence on the activities of the Fascist-type right. The left claims that its zeal in this respect leaves much to be desired.[19] The important point, however, is that the main activist challenge to the status quo in Britain, in all its diverse forms, from strike action to mass demonstrations, comes from organized labour and the left, and it is this, rather than the activities of the Fascist-type right, which occupies the police and preoccupies those who control it.

It is the 'extreme' left in particular which has traditionally been the main focus of attention of the coercive agencies and the security services. This antedates the Russian Revolution, but it is after 1917 that the struggle against Communism in Britain – and in the Empire – began in earnest. The installation of a Communist regime in Russia, to which the British Communist Party was closely linked, gave to the struggle a

[19] For recent claims to this effect, see for instance P. Hain (ed.), *Policing the Police*, vol. i (1979) and vol. ii (1980). For an earlier period, see R. Kidd, *British Liberty in Danger* (1940).

national and patriotic veneer which also provided a very useful additional element of legitimation: what was being fought, it was claimed, was not a set of people with extreme left-wing views as such, but men and women who were for all practical purposes the agents of a foreign power. What these people might say about their allegedly socialist aims for Britain could thus be discounted as a mere cover for sinister, Moscow-inspired, and anti-British activities. Not all such people were necessarily of evil intent; but those who were not could be regarded as mere dupes.

In the years following the First World War and the foundation of the Communist Party, Communists were subjected to severe harassment, with raids on party offices and gaol sentences on flimsy charges. Albert Inkpin, the party's Secretary, was arrested in 1921 and sentenced to six months hard labour on charges under the Defence of the Realm Act. In 1925, twelve leading Communists were arrested and tried on charges of uttering and publishing seditious words and libels, and of incitement to mutiny (under the Incitement to Mutiny Act of 1797). Five of the defendants who had previous political convictions received a one-year sentence, and the seven others got six months. The character of the trial may be judged from the remark of the judge to those accused who had no previous convictions: 'Those of you who will promise me that you will have nothing more to do with this association or the doctrine which it preaches, I shall bind over to be of good behaviour in the future. Those of you who do not will go to prison.'[20] The wickedness of the accused is well demonstrated by the fact that they refused to avail themselves of this generous offer. The sentences very conveniently kept them all in gaol during the General Strike.

Police attention, then and later, was also devoted to other left-wing organizations, such as the Communist-led National Unemployed Workers' Movement: the NUWM, it has been noted,

received constant and often disruptive attention from the police: it was kept under constant surveillance both by the Special Branch and by informers inside the organisation, its leader was eventually arrested at a critical point in the campaign, its demonstrations were certainly dealt with in a fairly tough manner, and its offices were searched and its documents confiscated, an action for which the NUWM was later awarded damages in court.[21]

Communist and other left-wing activists in Britain were not hanged,

---

[20] S. Shetreet, *Judges on Trial* (1976), p. 171.
[21] J. Stevenson, 'The Politics of Violence', in G. Peele and C. Cook (eds.), *The Politics of Reappraisal 1918–1939* (1975), p. 161. See also W. Hannington, *Never On Our Knees* (1967). Hannington was the National Organizer of the NUWM.

tortured, or sentenced to long terms of imprisonment on trumped-up charges; and the reference in the above quotation to 'damages in court' shows well enough that the left was not ultimately deprived of recourse to the law, however unjust the application of the law might often be. These are not small matters; and they need to be noted, since they have formed an integral part of the process of containment. But so has it to be noted that capitalist democracy in Britain has always been perfectly compatible with the harassment of activists, and the prosecution and punishment of Communist and other such political nonconformists. Nor would it do to ignore the fact that police and military activity in Ireland and territories under colonial rule was always much less restrained than in Britain.[22]

With the growth of the left since the Second World War, the attempt to contain and control its activists assumed ever more extensive and systematic forms. With every decade that has passed, the policing function undertaken by the state has become ever more elaborate, and is further enhanced by economic crisis and the social tensions which crisis generates.

In such circumstances, a great deal happens which affects the character and workings of capitalist democracy. Some people die in custody in unexplained circumstances.[23] Some others, more fortunate, are only beaten up.[24] In some areas, coloured immigrants, particularly young

[22] Never less so than in Ireland in 1919–20, when the Royal Irish Constabulary and the 'Black and Tans' took the law into their own hands and answered attacks against them by indiscriminate revenge against Irish people. For the British Government's support of their activities, see T. Jones, *Whitehall Diary* (ed. K. Middlemas, 1971). Dr Middlemas speaks of this period as having produced 'the most ruthless coercion in recent imperial history' (p. xxi).

[23] In a letter to the Home Secretary at the beginning of 1980, Michael Meacher, MP, noted that there had been '245 deaths in police custody in England and Wales since 1970, including 143 from non-natural causes, or about 15 a year (rising from three in 1970 to 30 in 1978). In nearly 10 per cent of the cases (23 out of 245) there was apparently no inquest . . . even though it had repeatedly been said that no investigation was necessary because there was always an inquest.' (*The Times*, 7 January 1980) In a letter to Mr Meacher, the Home Secretary confirmed that there had been 245 deaths in police custody and noted that inquests had been held in 223 of the 245 cases (*The Times*, 9 January 1980).

[24] In 1979, the Report of the Police Complaints Board noted that there had been 13,079 complaints from the public in 1978 against the police, 2,483 of which concerned 'assault' and 2,523 'irregularity of procedure'. The Board recommended disciplinary action against the officer involved in fifteen cases, and more than a 1,000 officers were warned or advised about what was considered unreasonable behaviour (*Report of the Police Complaints Board*, HMSO 1978, quoted in the *Guardian*, 24 May 1979). In 1981, the number of complaints was 16,789, and the Board recommended disciplinary action on thirty-nine of the charges (*Report of the Police Complaints Board*, HMSO 1982, quoted in the *Guardian*, 7 April 1981).

blacks, are subject to much police harassment. The technology of surveillance makes daily progress, and the area of surveillance is steadily widened.[25] Increasingly, army officers turn their gaze homewards, and study riot control, 'counter-insurgency', and 'low intensity operations'.[26]

Wrong-doing by the coercive agencies of the state in the course of enforcing 'law and order' or in their other pursuits occasionally focuses attention upon their abuse of power. But the attention is in some ways misdirected. The police, the surveillance agencies, and the military are always liable to misuse the power they have. But it is their political superiors who give them that power; and it is prime ministers, home secretaries, and other responsible ministers who shield the people concerned from criticism, challenge, and investigation. Even police states are not usually run by policemen; and it is civilians and elected governments, in a capitalist democracy such as Britain, who largely determine what the police and the military do, and how they do it. It is only in extreme cases that home secretaries have ventured to depart from their normally unswerving and unqualified defence of the forces of law and order; and when judges have been called upon to inquire into episodes where policemen and soldiers were alleged to have been guilty of offences ranging from brutality to murder, they too have always surrounded what mild criticism they might have with every possible qualification and extenuation. The solidarity of different parts of the state system is in this instance very impressive, and also very detrimental to the placing of effective checks on the coercive agencies. For solidarity is here akin to complicity; and complicity breeds abuses.

[25] A Labour M.P. recalled in the House of Commons in 1978 that, in 1975, Lord Harris of Greenwich, then a Minister of State at the Home Office in Harold Wilson's Government, had defined political activity coming within the purview of the Special Branch as 'activities which threaten the safety or wellbeing of the state and are intended to undermine or overthrow parliamentary democracy by political, industrial or violent means'. The MP then asked the Home Secretary, Merlyn Rees, whether he was aware that 'under the present definition it includes those attending anti-apartheid meetings and those who enrol as students with the Workers' Educational Association'. The Home Secretary did not deny this, and said that he had reminded 'the police force concerned that I was, and indeed would be happy again to be, a tutor in the WEA . . .' (*The Times*, 7 April 1978). In February 1980, it was disclosed that Dame Judith Hart had had her phone tapped by the security services in 1974, while she was a minister in the Wilson Government. 'I think it would be understandable if the Morning Star and Communist Party phones were being tapped,' she said, 'but I would like to know that the National Front's phones are tapped as well.' (The *Guardian*, 4 February 1980.) On police and surveillance activities, see, e.g., Hain, *Policing the Police*. For the Special Branch, see T. Bunyan, *The Political Police in Britain* (1976).
[26] See, e.g., C. Ackroyd, K. Margolis, J. Rosenhead, and T. Shallice, *The Technology of Political Control* (1977).

While the 'loyalty' of governments towards the forces of law and order never wavers, there have been occasions when the loyalty of servants of the state towards governments has in effect lapsed. Spying for a foreign power is of course the extreme example of such a lapse; but there have been less extreme instances which are interesting and significant. Two such instances may be briefly noted here.

One of them, the Curragh 'Mutiny', concerned the response of military personnel (and others) to the attempt of the Liberal Government of Herbert Asquith in the years immediately preceding the First World War to bring Ulster into Home Rule for Ireland. Lord Blake has noted about this episode that 'we find Privy Councillors recommending rebellion, former Law Officers of the Crown urging armed resistance to an Act of Parliament, prominent soldiers disregarding their oaths of secrecy, and Bonar Law himself, leader of the Tory Party, seriously considering whether to encourage a mutiny in the Army';[27] and he also observes that 'it was clear by the end of 1913 that, quite apart from any move in the House of Lords to amend the Mutiny Act, the Army might prove a broken reed if the Government tried to coerce Ulster'.[28]

In the event, there was no 'mutiny' over Ulster, and British officers were not actually put to the test of whether they would obey a government whose legitimacy was not in question but whose policies on this issue they found unacceptable. But enough was said and done at the time to show — if demonstration were needed — that people in the service of the state will, in some circumstances, not only disobey the government of the day but will also actively seek to subvert it. This is no matter for surprise: it is rather the notion of total and unqualified or automatic obedience which seems bizarre. Faced with policies and actions which they find utterly abhorrent, men and women in positions

---

[27] R. Blake, *The Unknown Prime Minister* (1955), p. 121. At a rally at Blenheim Castle on 29 July 1912, Bonar Law said that the Liberal Government of Mr Asquith might carry the Home Rule Bill through the House of Commons, 'but when then? I said the other day in the House of Commons and I repeat here that there are things stronger than Parliamentary majorities', and Bonar Law also said, 'I can imagine no length of resistance to which Ulster can go in which I should not be prepared to support them' (ibid., p. 130).

[28] Ibid., p. 178. Note also Lord Blake's remark that Major-General (later Field Marshal) Sir Henry Wilson, who as at the time Director of Military Operations at the War Office, 'seems to have regarded it as quite compatible with his official duties to pass confidential information to the Leader of the Opposition, where such information might be of value in the struggle against Home Rule' (ibid., p. 179). Wilson, he also notes, 'was well acquainted with the military preparations in Ulster and gave advice to the Ulster volunteers, visiting Belfast for that purpose early in 1914' (ibid., p. 180).

of responsibility and power will oppose them and seek to defeat the government which pursues them; and the more abhorrent the policies, the greater will be the lengths to which these men and women will be willing to go.

Another episode, which makes the same point, has attracted much less attention, possibly because the purposes that were sought by 'disloyal' servants of the Crown were so thoroughly vindicated by subsequent events. This is the passing of secret information to Winston Churchill in the thirties, when he was the leading figure opposing the policies of appeasement of Conservative governments. Churchill's biographer, Martin Gilbert, has noted that 'more than twenty civil servants and government officials', 'alarmed by what they considered to be the dangerous neglect of Britain's national interest, took the initiative in going to see him, or in sending him secret material'.[29] Gilbert also writes that 'serving officers and senior civil servants felt driven to seek him out, knowing full well that it was a breach of the Official Secrets Act to do so, but confident that their secrets would be safe in his hands, and that he would use them in what he and they regarded as the national interest'.[30] It may be taken for granted that, except for people who pass secret information for money or under blackmail or for some other personal reason, those who do are indeed always seeking to serve what they conceive to be the 'national interest'. The trouble, of course, is that the 'national interest' is not a mathematical formula, susceptible to irrefutable proof, but a matter of interpretation admitting diametrically opposed conclusions. There are very few actions which cannot be brought within its fold with at least some degree of plausibility. In the present context, what matters is that servants of the Crown do at times find themselves in disagreement with the government of the day as to what constitutes the 'national interest': what they do about this must depend upon many different circumstances, including the importance of the issue and the depth of the disagreement. What is not reasonable is to expect them never to disobey the government and act against it.

---

[29] M. Gilbert, *W. S. Churchill. 1922-1939* (1976), vol. v, p. xxi.

[30] Ibid., p. 884. Gilbert also quotes the letter of rebuke which Sir Maurice (later Lord) Hankey, the Secretary of the Cabinet, wrote to Churchill, and which shows awareness that leaks were occurring of which Churchill was the recipient (pp. 878 ff.). The whole of ch. 43, 'Information in the Public Interest' is particularly relevant to the question at issue here.

IV

The qualities for which judges in Britain have been most highly praised are their independence and impartiality — independence from the government of the day and other sources of pressure; and impartiality towards those appearing before them. And indeed, judges have been mostly independent of the government and of other pressures; and they have at least striven to be impartial. In regard to the management of class conflict and the containment of pressure from below, however, the matter is rather more complicated. For judges have in this respect played an exceedingly conservative role. This may not affect the notion of independence: judges have not had to be subjected to pressure to play this role. But it does affect the notion of impartiality: in the struggle between the forces of conservatism and the forces of reform and change, judges have tended to be quite solidly on the side of the former against the latter.

This has a lot to do with who judges are. They are mostly drawn from the same narrow segment of the population from which is also recruited the majority of people who exercise power in Britain; and they similarly tend to be educated at public schools and at Oxford or Cambridge.[31] Moreover, their professional background as barristers is hardly conducive to radicalism. The profession is notoriously conservative, and barristers who are radical do not become judges. What this means is that the spectrum of thought in which judges dwell is at least as narrow as that of other people of power, probably more so. But judicial partisanship in the area specified is not only a matter of social provenance or professional background: much of it is inherent in the performance of the judicial function in a class-divided society such as Britain.

As in the case of civil servants, the outlook of judges would matter a lot less than it does if they did not wield a great deal of power. Judges do much more than 'apply' the law as they find it; they interpret it and therefore shape it, often with very large consequences. In this task of interpreting the law, judges not uncommonly see themselves as the guardians of the social order against anyone, including ministers, who seeks to change it in ways which they find unacceptable. In a famous judgement in 1961, Lord Simonds expressed this notion of guardianship as follows:

I entertain no doubt that there remains in the courts of law a residual power to enforce the supreme and fundamental purpose of the law,

---

[31] J. A. G. Griffith, *The Politics of the Judiciary* (1977), pp. 24 ff.

to conserve not only the safety and order but also the moral welfare of the State, and that it is their duty to guard against attacks which may be the more insidious because they are novel and unprepared for ... The same act will not in all ages be regarded in the same way. The law must be related to the changing standards of life, not yielding to every shifting impulse of the popular will but having regard to fundamental assessments of human values and the purposes of society.[32]

The case in question concerned the publication of a booklet, the *Ladies Directory*, which consisted of advertisements by prostitutes. But Lord Simonds's words are clearly applicable to other situations, indeed to almost any situation. Fifteen years later, Lord Denning, then Master of the Rolls, wrote of the 'notable advance during the past two decades of the doctrine of judicial review of executive acts', and specified that 'the essence of the doctrine is that all power, however plenary in form, is given for a purpose and that, if it is exercised for any other purpose it is absurd. So if the exercise is challenged, a court of law must inquire whether the minister acted from an improper motive or otherwise in bad faith.' Also, 'the minister must get his law right'; and he must also 'direct himself properly on the facts'.[33]

Such claims and stipulations provide the courts with an almost limitless area of discretion. Some judges seek to exercise greater discretion, some less. But the important point is that what is involved here *is* judicial discretion, inevitably instilled with the conservative presumptions of judicial thinking. This is particularly evident in judicial attitudes to the rights of property, to trade unions, and to what might be called the rights of the state.

The pressure for reform naturally involves a challenge to the rights of property and aims at the erosion of privilege of one sort or another. Class conflict cannot be defined in these terms alone; but they constitute much of its substance. In that conflict, property and privilege have always found judges to be amongst their most vigilant and dedicated defenders. Lord Devlin has suggested a rationale for this position: 'Change, in the measure of its beneficence to the many, causes hardship and displacement to the few. It is essential to the stability of society that those whom change hurts should be able to count on even-handed justice calmly dispensed, not driven forward by the agents of change.'[34] This sounds reasonable. Unfortunately, the judicial concern for 'those whom change hurts' has been exceedingly selective throughout history. Those whom it has protected have been the owners of property rather

[32] *Shaw* v. *Director of Public Prosecutions*, in Griffith, *Politics*, p. 137.
[33] *The Times*, 27 October 1976.
[34] P. Devlin, *The Judge* (1979), p. 9.

than the propertyless; and the 'agents of change' whom the judges have sought to control and constrain have usually been governments and public authorities driven to curb the rights of property and the prerogatives of capital. Since the Second World War, judges have had to accept a greater degree of 'interference' by the state in these rights and prerogatives, and a much greater degree of intervention also in economic and social areas in which the state was previously much more reluctant to enter. But they have nevertheless remained among the most resolute opponents of reform.

Many local authorities under Labour control have wished to act as 'agents of change'; but they have had to reckon with a highly restrictive judicial view of what they could do. Judges have often been called upon to decide whether a local authority had acted 'reasonably'. But what is 'reasonable' is more often than not a matter in which ideological dispositions must enter; and the ideological dispositions of judges have again and again led them to interpret in highly conservative terms what it is reasonable for local authorities to do. Their ideological dispositions do not *always* produce conservative decisions; but they strongly *tend* towards them. The Law Lords' decision in January 1982 that the Labour-controlled Greater London Council was not empowered to levy a supplementary rate in order to pay for a 25 per cent reduction in fares on buses and underground trains is a prime example of such decisions. Much of the case turned on the meaning to be attached to the duty laid on the GLC by the London (Transport) Act of 1969 to provide 'integrated, efficient and economic transport facilities and services for Greater London'. But as Lord Scarman said in his judgment, 'as a matter of English usage, the term "economic" (as also the noun "economy") has several meanings . . . It is a very useful word: chameleon-like, taking its colour from its surroundings.' The point is that the colour which the judicial eye greatly tends to favour is one or other shade of blue, not pink, let alone red.

Trade unions are also 'agents of change'; and they too have always found the courts in their path. Unions seek to limit the rights of employers and of property in general; and to extend the rights of labour. Governments seeking to manage class conflict have been compelled to endorse many such rights and to give them legal sanction; and thereby to accept, with however many reservations, various forms of trade-union activism and industrial militancy. The courts have traditionally been very unsympathetic to the affirmation of trade-union rights, and deeply hostile to trade-union militancy; and they have lost few opportunities to limit the scope of the concessions made to the unions by

governments and Parliament, or to annul them. The history of 'industrial relations' is strewn with judicial decisions in one way or another adverse to the unions, and which have been left for governments to undo. 'It is no exaggeration to say', in the words of one writer, 'that with the exception of wartime laws and the 1927 Trade Disputes Act every significant statute bearing on industrial disputes in the century after 1870 was the result of judicial decisions which had nullified the intended effect of previous legislation.'[35] In all these decisions, the judges were totally 'independent' of employers; nor can it be said that their purpose was to help employers against wage-earners. Their purpose was to apply the law as they saw it. But the result of what they saw as being the law has always tended to be of great help to employers, to owners of property, and to conservative forces in general.

The judges have been particularly helpful to the state, when the issue was one that could be construed as involving 'national security'. In a classic (minority) opinion delivered in 1942, Lord Atkins expressed his 'apprehension' at the attitude of judges who 'when face to face with claims involving the liberty of the subject show themselves more executive-minded than the executive'; and he recalled that it had 'always been one of the pillars of freedom . . . that the judges are no respecters of persons and stand between the subject and any attempted encroachment on his liberty by the executive, alert to see that any coercive action is justified in law'.[36] In relation to 'national security' at least, the apprehension is well justified. For judges have generally been very willing to give to the state all the help it wanted in cases that could be claimed to involve the safety of the realm or any similar consideration. Judicial bias on this score was expressed with the utmost clarity by Lord Denning, sitting with two fellow judges in the Court of Appeal in 1977, to hear the appeal of Mark Hosenball, an American journalist, against the dismissal by the Divisional Court of his appeal for an order of *certiorari* to quash the Home Secretary's decision to have him deported because, it was said, he had obtained 'for publication information harmful to the security of the United Kingdom'. No evidence was produced, but the Court of Appeal upheld the dismissal, and Lord Denning made the following remarks in the course of his judgement:

If it was a case where the ordinary rules of natural justice had to be observed some criticism could be made of the Home Secretary. It could be said that Mr Hosenball had not been given sufficient information to

---

[35] M. Moran, *The Politics of Industrial Relations* (1977), p. 9.
[36] *Liversedge* v. *Anderson*, in Griffith, *Politics*, p. 79.

enable him to meet the charge against him. But it was no ordinary case. It was a case in which national security was involved. When the state was in danger, our own cherished freedoms, and even the rules of natural justice had to take second place : . . . In cases such as the present, where national security was involved, our rules of natural justice might have to be modified.[37]

There is no reason to believe that Lord Denning and his colleagues had themselves any evidence about the case, or knew that 'the state was in danger' and that 'national security' was truly involved. But they were entirely willing to trust Merlyn Rees, the (Labour) Home Secretary. As Lord Denning also said:

there was a conflict between the interests of national security and the freedom of the individual. The balance between the two was not for a court of law but for the Home Secretary. He was the person entrusted by our constitution with the task . . . In the present case the court had been assured that the Home Secretary himself had given the case his personal consideration and there was no reason to doubt the care with which he had considered the whole matter. He was answerable to Parliament for the way in which he did it and not to the courts.[38]

Judges do not always take so complacent a view of the activities of the executive, even in cases involving 'national security'. But while the state must expect the judiciary to be very strongly concerned with encroachments on the rights of property, it may well hope that the encroachments it makes on civic freedoms will meet with the sympathetic understanding of judges and with their support. It could hardly be otherwise with a body of people who have in common with the rest of the state the responsibility, as they see it, to help in the defence of 'stability'.

This defence of 'stability', and of conservative values in general, is not taken to be in the least 'partisan' or 'political'. On the contrary, the same fiction which is fostered about the 'non-political' nature of other parts of the state is also proclaimed, even more emphatically, in regard to judges. People with known and quite public previous affiliations (usually Conservative) are suddenly presumed to have become 'non-political' on their elevation to the bench, when all that this means is that they have ceased to be affiliated to a given political party and can no longer express a public preference for it. This is a rather narrow view of what being 'political' means.[39]

---

[37] *Regina* v. *Secretary of State for Home Department, Ex parte Hosenball, The Times* Law Report, 30 March 1977.   [38] Ibid.

[39] When a Labour MP referred to Lord Diplock as a 'Tory judge' in December 1980, the Speaker ruled that 'it is offensive to refer to a judge of the High Court

On the other hand, it is easy to see how convenient a fiction it is. For it is clearly of great value to the cause of 'stability', compliance, and conservatism in general, that as powerful an institution as the judiciary, so solidly embedded in the structure of power constituted by the state, should be thought to be altogether removed from the struggles proceeding in society, and should be held to be free from the ideological commitments which beset mere 'politicians' and other people. It is this presumption which has made High Court judges such useful chairmen and members of royal commissions, departmental committees, and particularly committees of inquiry into 'delicate' matters concerning the conduct of agents of the state, in cases where police violence, the killing of civilians by soldiers, etc., have occurred. The record shows that the state can, at the least, expect that the reports which are produced will say all that can possibly be said in favour of its agents. There may be no deliberate intention to 'white-wash'; but wrong-doing by the agents of the state is made to assume a very blurred and uncertain character.[40]

The insistence on the political independence of the judiciary has a powerful legitimating resonance; and it is all the more powerful because judges, however traditionally-minded they may be, do not always act as allies of the government and the state, even in cases which involve 'security'; and because no defendant, however antipathetic to the court, need take it for granted that his cause is lost in advance because of judicial animus. This is no small matter either. All the same, the bias remains, and constitues an important bulwark in the defence of the status quo.

V

The House of Lords and the monarchy also require mention here, since both are part of the machinery of containment embedded in the British political system. Although neither is now a vital element in the normal process of government, their political role is far from negligible,

---

by anything other than as a judge of the High Court'. 'Of course,' he also said, 'it is wrong for any of us to attribute to any judge a bias' (*The Times*, 19 December 1980).

[40] For a notable instance, see Lord Chief Justice Widgery's report on 'Bloody Sunday' in Londonderry in January 1972, when thirteen civilians were killed by paratroopers and a number wounded. See also the criticism of Lord Widgery's Report by Professor Samuel Dash, *Justice Denied* (1972), published by the International League for the Rights of Man and the National Council for Civil Liberties.

and can in circumstances of conflict and crisis become very considerable.

It has long been said that the House of Lords as at present constitued is an anachronism. The great majority of its members are hereditary peers, which is absurd. Admittedly, the majority of members who actually take an active part in the business of the Lords are not hereditary but life peers. However, these peers owe their presence in the House of Lords to appointment, and there is not much that is democratic about that either.

There are some obvious reasons for the survival of this kind of second chamber. One of them is that the Lords have undergone some measures of reform in this century: their power of delay of legislation was reduced to two years (and nullified in relation to major financial legislation) by the Parliament Act of 1911; and it was further reduced to one year by the Parliament Act of 1949. A further measure of reform was the institution of life peerages in 1958. These modifications have undoubtedly served to make the existence of the Lords an issue of less contention. Secondly, the Lords have been careful, ever since the crisis of 1910-11, to choose the ground on which to oppose the government of the day, and not to expose themselves to undue danger of drastic reform or even abolition; and they have found this all the easier because there have been very few occasions when a government has presented them with major measures of an utterly intolerable sort. Thirdly, there has been very little agreement on what further reform, of any substance, might be made. Finally, there has been very little impetus from either front bench for any such reform. Both Conservative and Labour leaders have not on the whole found much wrong with the Lords as they now are.

The political allegiance of the hereditary peers is overwhelmingly Conservative. For their part, the life peers mainly reflect the ideological dispositions of the Conservative and Labour front benches, which means that they span the familiar political range, from right-wing Conservative through Liberal to right-wing Labour. A few former left Labour MPs and others of a broadly similar outlook have also found their way into the peerage. But political views outside the conventional consensus are not much heard in the House of Lords, and are certainly not heard there to any effect. It is in fact a profoundly conservative chamber, well to the right of the House of Commons — one more forum for the expression of conventional views and reactionary prejudices, with ready access to extensive publicity. This is of course quite compatible with the claim which is often made for the House of Lords that it is a chamber rich with experience and eminence. On the other hand, it may

not be quite so compatible with the no less familiar claim that its debates are not only of 'high quality', but of higher quality than those of the House of Commons, since there is so much less 'partisan' strife in the House of Lords. What this really means is that debates in the Lords are mostly in the nature of minor variations on orthodox themes and conservative ideas. Whatever may be said about the level of debates in the House of Commons, they do at least reflect a more substantial range of ideas.

The House of Lords is said to perform an important function in the initiation and revision of legislation and other measures. But this is not simply a technical function: it often also has pronounced political connotations, and includes, whenever necessary, a stubborn and deter-mined defence of the rights of property and privilege against any serious encroachment. The House of Lords is no doubt many things; but it is above all another line of defence of conservatism and conservative forces in Britain.

The usefulness of the House of Lords to these forces may be illustrated by reference to a small but significant action which it took in 1979. On 1 February of that year, the House of Commons, on a free vote, resolved by 146 to 67 votes to set up a special commission on the subject of the breaches in oil sanctions against Rhodesia. The commission was to have access to cabinet papers, and its proposed brief was 'to consider, following the Bingham inquiry [published in September 1978], the part played by those concerned in the development and application of the policy of oil sanctions against Rhodesia with a view to deter-mining whether Parliament or Ministers were misled, intentionally or otherwise, and to report'.

The whole episode of oil sanctions against Rhodesia certainly represents one of the really major scandals in British political, administrative, and commercial history in the twentieth century.[41] When the Bingham Report was published, the *Sunday Times* wrote 'It appears that, for more than 12 years, two of our greatest companies, Shell and BP, have been pouring oil directly or indirectly into that supposed beleaguered economy, while officials and/or a clutch of senior Ministers either condoned their activities, shrugged their shoulders, or just did not bother to inquire how all Mr Smith's cars, tractors and lorries continued to drive ahead regardless,' and the paper also called for an 'inquest into deceit and dishonour'.[42] *The Times* for its part suggested

---

[41] For an account of the episode, beside the Bingham Report itself, see M. Bailey, *OilGate. The Sanctions Scandal* (1979).
[42] *Sunday Times*, 3 September 1978.

that 'the essential facts were known to officials, ministers and the Prime Minister himself . . . the Goverment of the day were consciously conniving in the circumvention of their own declared policy and law passed to defend this policy'.[43]

There were many other such expressions of indignation and condemnation, and demands for further action; and it might have been thought, at the very least, that further and more searching inquiries were necessary, not least because the episode appeared to cast so lurid a light on the conduct of so many highly placed people, and on the workings of much of the political system as well;[44] and this is not to speak of the dire consequences which the failure to bring Smith to heel had for the people of Rhodesia.[45] On the other hand, it may be that it is precisely because the issues were so grave and fraught that the notion of a commission, as proposed by the House of Commons, was soon buried. It was the House of Lords which did the burying. A week after the Commons vote, the Lords declined by 102 votes to 58 to support the Commons resolution. Michael Foot, then Leader of the House of Commons, then announced that the Government would not be deterred, and that it would 'come forward with proposals for dealing with the situation'. But the Government never did; and it was replaced in May 1979 by the Conservatives, whose Attorney-General was able to announce in December that there would be no further investigation, and no prosecutions for breaches of oil sanctions. It may well be that the proposed commission would have got nowhere, given the hedgehog-

---

[43] *The Times*, 7 September 1978. In a letter to *The Times* some weeks later, a Conservative MP, Hugh Fraser, wrote about the Royal Navy's ten-year blockade of the port of Beira that 'evidence now seems to show that after May, 1966, no tanker seriously sought access to Beira, because Shell and BP had closed down their tank farms; because after 1970 the port of Beira had so silted up as to be useless to major vessels; and because, from the first, oil products went unimpeded into Lourenco Marques' (*The Times*, 16 November 1978). The cost of the Beira Patrol was probably over £100 million.

[44] In his Introduction to Mr Bailey's book, Anthony Sampson notes that it provides 'sharp glimpses into the ways by which civil servants are able to dominate their Ministers, and to collaborate with the executives of multi-national corporations . . . the oil companies were able to keep contact with the civil servants on a "personal" basis – which meant in effect that the Ministers were not informed'; and the book, he also notes, show 'how civil servants were dependent on the oil companies for their information, and subservient to their viewpoint; and how some influential civil servants later joined the oil industry' (Bailey, *Oilgate*, p. 9).

[45] 'If oil supplies to Rhodesia had been even partially reduced for any length of time the HMS Tiger and Fearless talks in 1966 and 1968 would hardly have failed, and tens of thousands of Rhodesian lives would have been saved.' (A. Phillips, 'Oil Sanctions: will the Government shelve the Bingham report?, *The Times*, 3 December 1979).

like capacity of the official world to close in at any sign of danger.[46] But it was clearly useful to have the House of Lords as a means of defence against democratic intrusion.

The House of Lords is not as strong a line of defence as it used to be; and it knows that it would run great risks if it challenged the major legislative proposals of a government with a strong majority in the House of Commons, particularly in the earlier part of a government's tenure of office. But to speak here of 'a government' is misleading: it is a government putting forward left-wing measures (or considered such by the Lords) which is in question. Occasions may well arise when great risks appear worth taking; and the challenges which the House of Lords can issue to a government with a majority in the House of Commons can assume different forms, from outright opposition to a more qualified rejection, in a wearing-down process which is not spectacular or dramatic, but which can be effective. Nor is there any strong constitutional reason why the House of Lords should not seek to cause great difficulties to a government with a strong majority whose measures it found altogether detrimental to the 'national interest'; and it would be a government of the left rather than one of the right whose measures it would thus find detrimental.

The same point applies even more to a government which does not enjoy a comfortable majority in the House of Commons. So long as this was a Conservative government, its lack of a majority would not greatly trouble the Lords. On the contrary, they would want to help it on its way. It is when a government of the left lacks a parliamentary majority that the House of Lords discovers a democratic vocation, and affirms its right to strike down government legislation. This is what happened in 1974, when a minority Labour government came to office, and when the Lords rejected or drastically amended a whole series of government measures. What is sauce for the Conservative goose is definitely not sauce for the Labour gander. Any government, with or without a parliamentary majority, which seeks to implement radical or socialist measures in home policy, or defence, or foreign policy, must always confront a large coalition of conservative interests and forces: the House of Lords is quite naturally a part of that coalition, and able to play a very useful role in it.

---

[46] The announcement led Mr Gordon Wilson, a Scottish National Party MP, to say, rather pertinently, that 'it must now be believed that if Mr Nixon had been head of state in the United Kingdom, sheltered by the Establishment, he would have got off scott free' (*The Times*, 20 December 1979).

Even its most ardent defenders do not claim that the House of Lords is 'above politics', or 'politically neutral'. But such are precisely the terms in which the monarchy is usually discussed. There are many reasons why the claim that the monarchy is 'above politics' must be reckoned to be false.

To begin with, the values which the monarchy is agreed to personify are heavy with conservative connotations. The Queen is said to be the symbol of tradition, continuity, the nation, and so forth. But these are solid conservative notions, which glorify stability, gradualism, and the obliteration, at least in sentiment and rhetoric, of divisions of class, and any other division that might pose a threat to the status quo. No theme, in this century, has been more insistently affirmed, in connection with the monarchy, than the supposed 'unity of the nation', the idea that it is a 'family', which may have its difficulties and squabbles, but which is essentially one, represented in the person of the Queen, and also by her own family. What actual impact this has on the working class is perhaps less clear than might be suggested by the interest which is shown in the doings of the Royal Family, or even by the affection which many of its members appear to generate. But the intention (apart from the hard-headed wish to sell newspapers and magazines) is clearly to foster feelings of 'loyalty', patriotism, unity, 'moderation', reverence for tradition, military valour, an imperial heritage, and whatever else may help reduce the danger of working-class alienation from the political and social system.

The Queen and her family are at the top of the social ladder; and they must be expected to hold the views and prejudices associated with very rich landed aristocrats and other members of the uppermost layers of the upper classes. They do not normally make direct and explicit 'political' statements; but there need be no great doubt that their own political spectrum ranges from extreme conservatism to mild 'liberalism'.[47] None of these attitudes, it may be worth adding, is in the least incompatible with solicitude for the poor and the needy.

How important are the monarch's political inclinations in relation

[47] The Duke of Edinburgh in particular has not infrequently been moved to give public expression to his political philosophy. In 1977, for instance, he was lamenting the fact that while, a hundred years ago, people knew what to do – 'go out, work hard, earn a living, provide for his children, provide for health, provide for old age, leave something solid for his children, accumulate some wealth and some treasure of various kinds', all this was now apparently impossible: the state had taken over, and 'You must not accumulate wealth (well, it is not a question of must not, but it is so arranged that you should not)' (*The Times*, 18 January 1977).

to her constitutional functions? In Bagehot's classical formulation, the Queen has the right to be consulted, the right to encourage, and the right to warn. What this means in practice is that the monarch's office is a constant source of advice, admonition, and complaint; and this will inevitably be strongly coloured by the monarch's ideological dispositions and those of her own court advisers, whose minds are not likely to run in strongly radical directions either. In the normal run of business, this may not have much effect on the conduct of affairs. Prime ministers, and ministers, must listen to what the monarch says; but they are not obliged to take it very seriously. At least, the prime minister is not. But there are many different circumstances in which the monarch may intervene much more effectively than by the mere expression of opinions, and where Bagehot's formulation is quite inadequate to describe the monarch's role.

The crisis of 1931 provides a good example of how important and even decisive that role can be.[48] Attention has usually fastened, in the development of that crisis, on Ramsay MacDonald's own role and on his transformation from Labour Prime Minister into the Prime Minister of a 'National Government' in which the Conservatives had a predominant place. But King George V played a crucial part in making this outcome possible. MacDonald might well have resigned and left Baldwin to succeed him but for the insistence of the King that he must carry on, that he was 'the only man to lead the country through the crisis', and that he must reconsider his position.[49] MacDonald's recent biographer has noted that the King urged him to stay on as Prime Minister on three separate occasions, and did so on the third occasion 'in language that suggested that resignation would be tantamount to desertion'.[50] Marquand also suggests that 'the King's appeal turned the scales', and this is quite possible.[51]

---

[48] The political crisis which erupted in August 1931 was due to the fact that Ramsay MacDonald, the Labour Prime Minister, was unable to persuade a substantial number of his cabinet colleagues (or the TUC) to give final approval to the cuts in unemployment benefits and other 'economy' measures which he and Philip Snowden, the Chancellor of the Exchequer, wanted to carry through. MacDonald then formed a 'National Government'. At the General Election of October 1931, Labour was reduced to 52 seats (from 289) and the Conservatives won 471 seats, as compared to 260 in 1929.

[49] D. Marquand, *Ramsay MacDonald* (1977), p. 635.

[50] Ibid., p. 639.

[51] Ibid., p. 636. Leo Amery recorded that 'to be told by the King that he was the only man who could save England, and that the Conservatives and Liberals would support him in restoring the confidence of the world in the financial stability of the country, made an irresistible appeal to his vanity.' (L. S. Amery, *My Political Life* (1955), iii. 60.

The King's insistence is not difficult to understand. He had been advised, notably by Herbert Samuel, the Liberal leader, that 'in view of the fact that the necessary economies would prove most unpalatable to the working classes, it would be in the general interest if they could be imposed by a Labour Government'; but that it would in any case be best if MacDonald remained Prime Minister, whatever government was in office.[52] Nothing could have been more calculated to dishearten and reduce Labour opposition to the 'economy' measures that were being proposed; and the subsequent General Election, in which MacDonald led a 'National' coalition against Labour was a disaster for the Labour Party. This was not what the King had deliberately sought; but it was a result which his intervention certainly helped to bring about. And it was brought about without the King ever having departed from his 'neutral' constitutional position, 'above politics'.

In any case, the monarch's constitutional powers remain a matter of remarkable uncertainty in areas of crucial importance. Thus, the choice of a prime minister has very seldom been a matter in which the monarch has, in the modern era, had any real say — 1931 was clearly a most exceptional case. But it is not difficult to envisage circumstances in which the Queen could play a much more substantial role than has normally been the case in this century. A general election which failed to produce a clear result, and which left three parties with a roughly similar share of seats in the House of Commons, would clearly give to the monarch a much greater degree of influence than has been the case with a two-party system; or at least, it could give to the Court a much greater degree of influence. The same could be said in circumstances where, a prime minister having resigned, no agreement could be reached on his or her successor by the party or parties concerned. Nor is the Queen constitutionally required to accept advice from an outgoing prime minister on who his or her successor should be: 'It is in fact generally accepted', it has been said, 'that the Monarch is not bound to accept ministerial advice in her selection of a Prime Minister'.[53]

Furthermore, there is no unqualified obligation on the part of the monarch to grant a dissolution to a prime minister who asks for one.

[52] H. Nicholson, *King George the Fifth* (1952), p. 641. Geoffrey Dawson, Editor of *The Times*, was one of the people who saw the uses to which the King could be put, and told the King's Private Secretary that George V should 'impress upon Ramsay that it was his business to get the country out of the mess and to dwell, with any flattery that he liked, upon the opportunity and the responsibility' (J. E. Wrench, *Geoffrey Dawson and Our Times* (1955), p. 291).

[53] G. Marshall and G. C. Moodie, *Some Problems of the Constitution* (1967), p. 50.

In 1974 Mr Edward Short, then Leader of the House of Commons, replied, to a question on the issue, that 'constitutional lawyers agreed that the Sovereign was not bound in all circumstances to grant a Prime Minister's request for a dissolution'.[54]

These are clearly very large powers; and whether they are used or not does not depend on any settled rule or convention, but on circumstances. In the episode to which reference has already been made, namely the Curragh 'Mutiny', we find Bonar Law and Lord Lansdowne (leader of the Conservatives in the House of Lords) seeking to persuade the King that 'the Constitution was in a state of suspense; that a dissolution was the only method of averting civil war; that, if Asquith declined to recommend a dissolution, the King had a right to dismiss him and send for someone else who would do so'.[55] These were desperate and even, in the circumstances, ridiculous counsels, and nothing came of them. But those who proffered such counsels were very senior politicians indeed, and it is just as well to take note of the fact that politicians (and others) do allow their thoughts, in circumstances which they take to be exceptionally grave, to stray far from the conventional constitutional path. Thus it was that a by now famous meeting was held in May 1968, at a time of great difficulty for the Wilson Government, between Mr Cecil King, then Chairman of the International Publishing Corporation, Lord Mountbatten, the Queen's uncle, Hugh (now Lord) Cudlipp, then Editorial Director of the *Mirror* group, and Sir Solly (now Lord) Zuckerman, then Chief Scientific Adviser to HM Government. At that meeting, according to Mr King's diary recollection:

Mountbatten said he had been lunching at the Horse Guards and that morale in the armed forces had never been so low. He said the Queen was receiving an unprecedented number of petitions, all of which have to be passed on to the Home Office. According to Dickie [i.e. Mountbatten] she is desperately worried over the whole situation. He is obviously close to her and she is spending the week end at Broadlands. He asked if I thought there was anything he should do. My theme was that there might be a stage in the future when the Crown would have to intervene: there might be a stage when the armed forces were important. Dickie should keep himself out of public view so as to have clean hands if either emergency should arise in the future. He has no wish to intervene anyway.[56]

[54] D. Butler and D. Kavanagh, *The British General Election of October 1974* (1975), p. 20.
[55] Blake, *Unknown Prime Minister*, p. 152.
[56] *The Times*, 3 April 1981. Cudlipp's recollection of the episode, as published in 1976, has King speaking of a coming crisis in which 'the Government would disintegrate, there would be bloodshed in the streets, the armed forces would be

In circumstances of great crisis, when a government, most likely of the left, is pursing courses which powerful and conservative-minded people deem to be utterly disastrous to the 'national interest' (and such people would undoubtedly include the Queen's personal advisers, who are part of the world of affairs), thoughts naturally turn to the monarch as one possible countervailing force among others. There is not much point in speculating how or when that force might be used; but it would not be reasonable to assume that it never would be, the more so since any intervention by the monarch would be presented as falling well within the framework of the Constitution, and indeed to be required for the fulfilment of the monarch's role as the ultimate 'guardian of the Constitution'. A request by a Labour prime minister that enough peers be created to achieve a Labour majority in the House of Lords, with the stated purpose of abolishing the second chamber, is only one case where strong resistance from the monarch could be expected. Nor does it seem extravagant to suppose that, even if this stage had been successfully negotiated, the actual legislative proposals for the abolition of the House of Lords would also encounter very stiff resistance from this as well as from many other quarters — to what point it is impossible to tell. In this sphere as in others, the business of containment — for this is what is ultimately involved — must be related to the given circumstances: the more dramatic and unusual the circumstances, the more dramatic and unusual are the forms which that business may assume.

This and related issues will be discussed further in the last chapter. In the next chapter, I disucss the question of containment at a very different level, namely as it occurs in and around local government.

---

involved. The people would be looking to someone like Lord Mountbatten as the titular head of a new administration, somebody renowned as a leader of men who would be capable, backed by the best brains and administrators in the land, to restore public confidence. He ended with a question to Mountbatten — would he agree to be the titular head of a new administration in such circumstances?' (H. Cudlipp, *Walking on Water* (1976), p. 326). According to Cudlipp's account, Zuckerman strongly repudiated the suggestion and Mountbatten agreed with him.

5. CLASS, POWER, AND LOCAL GOVERNMENT

It is only in recent years that a substantial body of work has been produced on local government in Britain in the perspective of conflicting class interests. Until the seventies, the subject was predominantly treated in terms of a series of problems which required solution by the application of greater knowledge, more efficient methods of organization, goodwill, or whatever. The most important of these problems appeared to be the conflicting claims of 'efficiency' and 'democracy', to which were linked a variety of other problems, such as the relation of central to local government, the size of areas, internal organization, finance, personnel, etc. How far the question of class pressures and the will to contain pressure from below might affect these issues was seldom considered, or even perceived. Nor has this ceased to be the case. The radical and Marxist-oriented work that has been done in the last decade or so has posed a genuine challenge to traditional modes of thought and discussion about local government; but it is a challenge that has often been ignored, and prevailing orthodoxies have remained well entrenched.[1]

Yet local government in Britain has always been part of the system of power, with different interests naturally concerned to use it to their advantage. Writers who would shun the notion of class power in relation to present-day local government have had no great difficulty in according it at least some importance in relation to the past, and the more remote the past the more generous the concession. There is not much argument against the view that local government before the Municipal Corporations Act of 1835, and for a long while after, was a bastion of the dominant forces in the country, and the means whereby landowning aristocrats, members of the gentry, businessmen, merchants, and professional men affirmed and sanctioned at local level the power which was more generally theirs. Elie Halévy refers to pre-nineteenth-century local government as a system 'by which a body of gentlemen, owning land of a yearly value of two hundred pounds or more, were endowed with extremely drastic powers of justice, police and administration';[2] and there is general agreement that, whatever else the system

---

[1] For an excellent account and critique of 'orthodoxies' in relation to local government, see John Dearlove, *The Reorganisation of British Local Government* (1979).

[2] E. Halévy, 'Before 1835', in H. J. Laski, W. I. Jennings, and W. A. Robson (eds.), *A Century of Municipal Progress* (1935), p. 23.

was intended to achieve, not the least of its purposes was to ensure that the property, power, and privileges of these same gentlemen and their class as a whole should not be disturbed.

However, the impression is strongly conveyed in writing on the subject that local government was wholly transformed in this respect by the vast economic, social, political, and other changes which came with the Industrial Revolution, since when the ineluctable advance of progress, reform, and democracy has been the order of the day. This is why, it is implied, rough notions like class, domination, interests, and the like, however suitable they might be to analysing local government in an earlier epoch, have become ever less relevant to its analysis in the second half of the twentieth century.

But this hardly follows. It is perfectly possible — and obviously necessary — to acknowledge that many transformations have occurred in local government, including reform and 'democratization', without in the least accepting the notion that class power and containment are now irrelevant to it. Reform, progress, and 'democratization' are themselves part of a context of class pressures; and that context remains crucial for the character and shape of local government, and for the ways in which its various problems are tackled, or perceived. The expectation of quite specific political advantage is itself a spur to reform. Thus, various arguments were advanced in favour of the reform of the government of London in 1963 by the Conservative Government: but an additional factor working for reform was, in the moderate words of Professor Richards, that 'action in London imposed virtually no strain on Conservative party loyalties. As the London County Council was commonly dominated by a Labour majority, a Conservative Cabinet had few political inhibitions about promoting change.'[3] There may be issues in local government which are purely 'technical' and 'administrative'; but they are very unlikely to be major issues. All such issues are most likely to have strong class connotations. Here as elsewhere, the people in charge may not be aware of that fact, and may believe that they are guided purely by 'professional' concerns, or that they are acting for the good of the community 'as a whole'. But however sincerely meant, such affirmations do not prevent decisions being taken which are class-related and class-bound.

Different and conflicting class forces are reflected in the composition of local councils. Even at the beginning of the twentieth century, 'it was normal for the chairman of the county council to be a peer or a

---

[3] P. G. Richards, *The Reformed Local Government System* (1980), p. 40.

member of a major landowning family; in the county boroughs the manufacturers and major tradesmen played the leading role in local affairs'.[4] In other words, an array of conservative forces, representing various forms of property, continued to dominate local councils and sought to ensure that the interests of ratepayers would be protected and services kept at a level congruent with that purpose, that is to say as low as could be managed.

It was with the emergence of organized labour as a political force, first with the Independent Labour Party and then with the Labour Party itself, that this conservative preponderance — amounting to a near-monopoly — came to be seriously challenged. In 1900, West Ham was still the only authority to have had a socialist majority; and there was at the time 'no contest at all at the elections in about 350 boroughs. Some seats, but not usually all seats, were fought in 140 boroughs. Again, some of these contests were not party political. At council elections, the parties were even less involved.'[5]

Not surprisingly, conservative forces found the challenge very unwelcome. There had been plenty of local politics before then, but politics in which labour was one of the contestants was something else. Mr Bulpitt has noted that 'it was really only after 1919 that the idea that the local Council was not a fit place for party politics became widespread. Very soon it became a popular debating point to be used against Labour in local politics.'[6] Those who sought to preserve the myth of 'no politics' in local government assumed a variety of 'neutral' labels under which to fight the interlopers, and carefully avoided a close identification with their natural political home, the Conservative Party. They fought the left as Ratepayers, Citizens, Progressives, Moderates, Independents, even Anti-Socialists, often no doubt in the conviction that they were simply upholding good management, common sense, and the good of all, and opposing irrelevant 'politics' in the town hall. As a speaker at a Rochdale Rate Action Association meeting put it in 1960: 'Get rid of them; get rid of politicians in the Council Chamber and you will save five shillings on your rates.'[7] Saving five shillings on the rates was clearly not 'politics'.

From the beginning of the century onwards, organized labour continued to make electoral progress at local level, and by 1939 'the

[4] B. Keith-Lucas and P. G. Richards, *A History of Local Government in the Twentieth Century* (1978), p. 15.
[5] Ibid., p. 112.
[6] J. G. Bulpitt, *Party Politics in English Local Government* (1967), p. 9.
[7] J. G. Bulpitt, 'Party Systems in Local Government', in *Political Studies*, xi (1963) (1), 12, n. 1.

Labour Party had majorities on the LCC, on the County Councils of Durham, Glamorgan and Monmouthshire, on eighteen out of seventy-nine County Boroughs, on twenty-five non-county boroughs in England and Wales, and on fourteen Burghs, large and small, in Scotland. It also controlled seventy-six Urban Districts, and seventeen out of the twenty-nine Metropolitan Boroughs.'[8] It was this continued extension and implantation of Labour in the country which compelled the Conservative Party to assume the main responsibility for the struggle against it, and to come out after 1945 as the main organized force against the left in local elections.

The class composition of councils has continued right up to the present to suggest how different were the interests each side represented. Councillors sitting under a Conservative, Ratepayer, Independent, or some such label, were drawn from a variety of occupations and walks of life ranging across the upper-middle–lower-middle-class spectrum – landowners, manufacturers, farmers, shopkeepers, professional and managerial people, middle-class men and women without occupation, and so on. On the Labour side, councillors have tended to be drawn from within a distinctly lower social range: professional and semi-professional people, but also trade-union officials, teachers, skilled workers. The division is clearly not a simple one of working-class versus middle-class, or property versus the lack of it. But when all qualifications have been entered (including the fact that women and younger people as well as workers have always been greatly under-represented in local government), it remains the case that the composition of councils has shown a very marked class differentiation as between Labour and the rest.

This has had a direct bearing on what councils choose to do. Local government is severely constrained by statute and by central government. But it nevertheless retains a degree of choice in the services it provides, the amenities it chooses to foster, and the provisions it makes for this or that group or class.[9] Given this element of choice, there has always been a marked difference between the attitudes and policies of Conservative and Conservative-inspired authorities on the one hand, and Labour ones on the other. Conservative-inspired councils

---

[8] G. D. H. Cole, *A History of the Labour Party Since 1914* (1948), p. 444.

[9] 'The timing, scope, funding and distribution of local government services is a matter which is far more within the scope of their powers than is commonly recognized in the literature of English local government. Examples of the variation of service can be found over the whole range of local government activity.' (N. T. Boaden and R. R. Alford, 'Sources of Diversity in English Local Government Decisions', in *Public Administration*, xlvii (1969), 204.

have traditionally sought to lighten rather than increase the financial burdens of ratepayers, property, and business; they have tended to look with a sceptical eye upon the extension of services and amenities, particularly free services and amenities; and they have stressed in their policies self-improvement rather than collective provision. By contrast, Labour authorities have had pronounced interventionist tendencies; they have sought the extension of services, day nurseries, amenities for old people, welfare services generally; and they have sought to make greater use of their permissive powers and been more generous in their spending policies, employed more social workers, favoured expenditure on the young, the poor, and immigrants. Of course, not all councils, whether Conservative or Labour, have been true to type; but they have nevertheless followed typical and contrasting modes of behaviour. Professor G. W. Jones makes the point for one city, Wolverhampton, which may serve more generally. He notes that in May 1967 Labour lost control of the Council and the Conservatives had a majority for the first time in fifteen years. He writes as follows:

The Conservative take-over was not simply a matter of a change of personnel at the top. Policies changed radically. Within twelve months of taking office the Conservatives reversed many Labour policies. They dismantled the Corporation's civic catering department and its direct-labour building department. They ran down the Corporation's experimental estate agency and decided to close the municipal sewage farm. Council houses were offered for sale to tenants, Council house rents were raised, a rent rebate scheme introduced, and tenants were allowed to build porches at their front doors. Corporation land was sold to housing associations for building. Labour's proposals for comprehensive education were revised to save the main Grammar schools, and a selective system of education was introduced into one area which had had comprehensive schools for twelve years.[10]

Conservative councils have always been much concerned to limit the field of public enterprise and to curb 'municipal socialism'. As J. L. Hammond put it for the nineteenth century, they worked on the principle that 'so long as private enterprise was left unchecked nothing could go wrong with social life, and that if the rights of property were ever threatened, everything would go wrong with it'.[11] This ideological bias found expression in the stubborn struggle against the 'municipaliz-ation' of such utilities as water, gas, and electricity;[12] and much the

[10] G. W. Jones, *Borough Politics* (1969), p. 346.
[11] J. L. Hammond, 'The Social Background 1835–1935', in Laski *et al, Municipal Progress*, p. 41.
[12] See, e.g. 'The Public Utility Services', in ibid.

same bias has also guided Conservative councils in all other realms of activity, even though they have been compelled to accept in the twentieth century (and came to find it 'natural' to accept) much more public intervention and collective provision than had been the case in the nineteenth.

The interventionist and 'collectivist' propensities of Labour authorities, by contrast, create a problem for all conservative forces, and for the state. From the last decades of the nineteenth century, and ever more so in the twentieth, local government has constituted one channel of popular pressure, and a means of asserting demands by way of elected institutions. As noted earlier, local government is the only part of the state system, beside the House of Commons, which is based on the elective principle: from the point of view of the conservative forces, this is precisely why it must be controlled and contained.

In *Representative Government* (1861), John Stuart Mill, following de Tocqueville, had insisted on the importance of local representative bodies for the 'public education of the citizens'; and he had also, more specifically, made the point that 'local functions, not being in general sought by the higher ranks, carry down the important political education which they are the means of conferring, to a much lower grade in society'.[13] These, and similar uses of local government, were well understood, then and later. In 1875 one writer spoke of local government as 'the permanent bulwark of social order', because, by 'accustoming representatives of all classes to work together daily for public but non-political objects,' it would 'strike at the root of . . . class prejudices', and help build up 'conservative barriers or breakwaters against revolutionary floodwaves'.[14] In introducing the Local Government (England and Wales) Bill in the House of Commons in 1893, the President of the Local Government Board said that local democratic institutions 'are not only good for the purposes for which they are devised but are good for the state'.[15] Some sixty years later, in a lecture delivered under the auspices of the Conservative Political Centre, J. H. Warren argued that 'in the local communities with which it is concerned, local government brings together men and women of very different creed, outlook and station in life, for practical cooperation in accepted tasks and interests';[16] and he also described local government as 'a great

[13] J. S. Mill, *Considerations on Representative Government* (World's Classics, 1912), p. 365.
[14] Dearlove, *Reorganization of Local Government*, p. 234.
[15] Ibid.
[16] J. H. Warren, *In Defence of Local Democracy* (1956), p. 8.

agency of reconciliation in our national life, taking much of the sharp edge of the war of class and creed. You do not bring men and women of every class, creed, and station in life into necessary cooperation in practical tasks without mutual adjustment of ideas and feelings . . .'[17] Such hopes and expectations were, however, dependent on local government remaining in 'moderate' hands, even if they now were in increasing number Labour hands. The point was to have both a genuine degree of local government and an effective measure of containment of it.

This has on the whole been very successfully achieved. Thousands upon thousands of men, and a good many women, found in local government a way of giving expression to their activist and reforming promptings; and the political system thus demonstrated that it was available to people who wanted to use it. In countless different ways, local councillors were able to make some contribution to the improvement of health, housing, educational, and other facilities in their area. The improvements might be small: but to those who were responsible for them, they were a visible sign that immediate activity for practical reform was not in vain.

Also, local government was one institution in the state system where working men and women were able to achieve direct participation in the making of decisions. No doubt, workers occasionally went from the work-bench to the House of Commons; but local government was much more accessible, and in addition to providing an opportunity to take part in government at local level, it gave status, prestige, honour, and influence to people who otherwise had very little or none of it. It is impossible to say how much local government thus helped to legitimate the political system as a whole. But in so far as it attracted into the system people who were almost by definition activists, its contribution to that legitimation cannot be taken to have been negligible.

Yet local authorities, including Labour authorities, have given very little trouble to central government. In 1980, Peter Saunders wrote of local government as the 'Achilles heel of the British political system'. This he explained was 'partly because of its specific mode of operation — it is relatively open to political pressures from non-capitalist interests'; but also, he added, 'because of its specific range of functions — i.e. it is oriented to the provision of services on criteria of need, and thus represents a potential challenge to the market and the commodity form on which capitalism is based'.[18] But the challenge has over the years

[17] Ibid., p. 12.
[18] P. Saunders, 'Local Government and the State', in *New Society*, 13 March 1980.

very seldom been strongly posed by local authorities. Two recent writers on British government have noted that 'the tone of most local authorities' discussions with central departments is one of co-operation and harmony rather than antagonism';[19] and two other writers have said in relation to local government in the post-war years that 'local authorities are law-abiding bodies. They do not engage in outright defiance of the state.'[20]

This is surely to raise a question rather than to answer it. That Conservative authorities should not have found much cause for opposition to governments concerned with the curtailment of public expenditure is not remarkable; there have only been a few exceptional issues – for instance comprehensive schooling – when Conservative authorities have had occasion to oppose the government with any great determination.[21] But Labour authorities have had many such occasions, ever since they came to establish a presence in local government and to control councils. Again and again they have been required to administer and execute policies to which they were strongly opposed, and to accept constraints which deeply offended their convictions. They were sometimes able to attenuate the rigours of the policies which they were required to administer. But they could not systematically ignore them, or act counter to them, without choosing to enter into conflict with central government. A good many tried, but soon desisted. A few, which would not give in, have made a mark on the history of local government in Britain.

The most notable of them is Poplar, which gave 'Poplarism' to the political language, and whose socialist councillors sought in the early twenties to provide somewhat more ample relief to the poor of the borough than was customary, and then refused to levy 'precepts' for outside authorities, particularly the London County Council. Their

[19] M. Beloff and G. Peele, *The Government of the United Kingdom: Political Authority in a Changing Society* (1980), p. 269.

[20] Keith-Lucas and Richards, *History of Local Government*, p. 177.

[21] In November 1975 the (Labour) Secretary of State for Education approved proposals for the reorganization of secondary education on comprehensive lines put forward by the Labour-controlled Tameside Council; and detailed arrangements were made for the change-over to come into effect in September 1976. In May 1976 the Conservatives won control of the Council and decided not to proceed with the plans. Under the powers given to him to issue directions to local education authorities if he was satisfied that they were acting unreasonably, the Secretary of State required Tameside to implement the plans, and the Divisional Court ordered it to comply. The Court of Appeal promptly overruled the Divisional Court and the Law Lords even more promptly upheld the Court of Appeal. For some pertinent comments on the Lords' judgment, see J. A. G. Griffith, 'The Tameside Opinion', in *New Statesman*, 29 October 1976.

actions brought them before the High Court and then to prison; but what they did also helped to bring about significant changes in local government administration and in the rate equalisation system.[22]

Another more recent rebellious council was the (Labour) Urban District Council of Clay Cross, in Derbyshire, which decided in 1972 not to implement any of the provisions of the new Housing Act of that year, and notably not to increase council-house rents. The councillors were duly surcharged. They appealed, lost in the High Court, were given fourteen days to pay, and disbarred from their positions as councillors. They in turn started proceedings against the Secretary of State and the District Auditor, lost, and appealed. In the High Court, Lord Denning and his fellow judges dismissed the appeal.[23]

These and other cases of defiance of central government and Parliament have been exceptional: 'Poplarism' has remained a relatively isolated phenomenon. Central government in Britain has never had to contend with a serious rebellion by Labour authorities. This is rather remarkable; and an explanation of the fact helps to illustrate further some important features of the political system in relation to local government, but also beyond it.

Any such explanation clearly has to begin with the power of central government to impose its wishes upon recalcitrant councils. The government does have at its disposal a large arsenal of financial, administrative, and coercive means to ensure compliance, and the courts can usually be relied on to act as a strong restraining force upon such councils.[24] For all the rhetoric about local democracy, citizen participation, and the like, local government in Britain is a greatly constrained and limited business. Central government can, at the limit, suspend councils and have their duties performed by its own commissioners. It can, by way of the 'surcharge' of councillors by unsympathetic auditors, bring about their personal ruin as well as their political demise. It can, more commonly, admonish and instruct. As governments have sought to cut expenditure and achieve retrenchment, so have they been concerned to extend their means of control and coercion over local authorities, and have been particularly concerned to do so because of the large and growing share of local expenditure as part of total public expenditure. No council can ever fail to be mindful of what central government can

[22] For 'Poplarism', see N. Branson, *Poplarism 1919-1925* (1979); and Keith-Lucas and Richards, *History of Local Government*, ch. 4.
[23] For an account of Clay Cross, see D. Skinner and J. Langdon, *The Story of Clay Cross* (1974).
[24] For a comprehensive survey, see J. A. G. Griffith, *Central Departments and Local Authorities* (1966).

ultimately do to it if it seeks to resist commands from the centre.

As I have already noted, however, the point can be pushed too far. John Dearlove notes that, too often, 'the central government's potential for control is equated with the actual extent and effect of control, and the result of this is to exaggerate the lack of local autonomy and to ignore ways in which local authorities may be able to resist even quite explicit directives from the central government'.[25] The point may be put somewhat differently: what is striking about the cases where central government has come into open confrontation with local authorities, and sought to compel them to do its will, is not how easily this has been achieved, but how laborious and protracted a process this has tended to be. No doubt, central government ultimately has its way; but getting its way is not always easy, may be politically embarrassing, and sometimes requires concessions being made. It is a very unequal battle, but not always a hopeless one: as Keith-Lucas and Richards note, with reference to the battles that Poplar Council fought before and after the First World War, 'Poplarism' shows 'how the action of individual local authorities may influence not only the politics of the day, but the whole climate of opinion within which legislation takes place'.[26]

If this can be said about the isolated authorities which have on occasion chosen to defy the government, one wonders how much more could have been achieved had the defiant authorities not been so isolated, and if central government had been confronted with twenty Poplars and an equal number of Clay Crosses. Important though the power of government is, other and additional reasons why such resistance should not have occurred must be sought.

One such reason is the influence of senior officials in local government. These officials, like their counterparts in the civil service, are professional people who see their job as quite 'unpolitical', but who are not at all minded to look with any favour on 'extreme' policies and actions, particularly if these are likely to involve 'unpleasantness' with central government; and such people naturally see their task as ensuring the smooth co-operation of their authorities with government, and as minimizing conflict with it and with well-established local interests, rather than risk encouraging conflict by unconventional behaviour. Their ideological position is most likely to range from moderate Conservatism to moderate Labourism, and their advice to councillors is most likely to be in the direction of caution, compliance, and reasonableness, and

---

[25] J. Dearlove, *The Politics of Policy in Local Government* (1973), p. 15.
[26] Keith-Lucas and Richards, *History of Local Government*, p. 65.

repudiation of anything that might run the risk of transgressing the strict bounds of what they take to be the powers of the authority. The influence of these officials obviously varies, but is nowhere negligible, and is often considerable: naturally so, given the volume of business to be dealt with, its complexity, and the reliance of councillors on official advice. 'Advice' in this context can easily turn into the effective government of the authority. In any event, the advice and influence of senior officials must be assumed to run in conservative directions, and councillors bent on radical and innovative courses must be prepared to encounter opposition, hostility, and possibly obstruction from their officials.

The emphasis of recent years on greater 'professionalism' and better management techniques in local government, and on the need to concentrate greater power in the hands of chief executives, is likely to reinforce the trend towards caution and 'moderation'. The Bains Report, published in 1972, which advocated greater control for officers and less for council members, and which has been described as an 'officers' charter', has been widely adopted.[27] Without strong political influences to counter managerial and professional conservatism, this is the bias that is encouraged. The chief executive has been described as being at 'the centre of a communications network which relates him to all aspects of council business and gives him access to a breath of knowledge which departmental heads *and elected members* lack. Once appointed he is internally irremovable. His influence can be greater than any of his professional colleagues or indeed than *any member of the council*.'[28] This is very unlikely to make for the encouragement of radical policies, and even less for any propensity to defiance of central government, however iniquitous its policies and commands may be.

The pressure to conform is supplemented from two further sources. One of them is Conservative opposition to radical courses from within the authority; and there may also be opposition to such courses within the Labour group itself from 'moderate' Labour members. Labour groups are seldom ideologically united: the familiar division between left and right is naturally found here as well, and Labour members on

[27] R. Hambleton, *Policy Planning and Local Government* (1978), p. 56. The author also notes that 'much of corporate planning practice has played down values and the expression of values through political argument . . . each stage of the policy process has, in practice, tended to ignore distributional aspects. It is hardly surprising, therefore, that corporate planning has not been noteworthy for its impact on urban deprivation and other major social issues.' (Ibid., pp. 65–6.)

[28] Lord Redcliffe-Maud and B. Wood, *English Local Government Reformed* (1974), p. 95. My italics.

the right of the political spectrum can act as a powerful restraining force on their left-wing colleagues.

The other source of opposition to radical policies is the pressure of outside interests, in the local area and beyond. Writing about Birmingham, Ken Newton has noted that 'in general, it seems that those sections of the population which have the most individual political resources, the middle and upper class, also have the best organizational resources to protect their interest. The cumulative inequalities which mark off different social strata appear to be reinforced by the cumulative inequalities of the world of voluntary organizations.'[29] This is obviously not peculiar to Birmingham. Dr Newton also notes the important fact that 'well-established organizations probably have easy access to decision-makers and, in many cases, have been incorporated in the decision-making machinery'.[30] More specifically, 'local government bureaucrats play a role in directing the process of group politics. They have an extensive set of links and ties with established groups, and groups and bureaucrats can often settle a matter of an administrative or technical nature to their mutual satisfaction.'[31]

The 'countervailing' power of less well-established groups, which may be taken to include most if not all radical and activist groups in the locality, is not generally such as to be very effective. Their resources are much smaller than those of well-established groups, and they not only have to run the gauntlet of unsympathetic officials and of Conservative councillors; they are also likely to be viewed as noisy nuisances or malevolent agitators by many Labour councillors. In their turn, left-wing pressure groups, locked in conflict with Labour councils, have tended to perceive Labour councillors as being part of an alien and hostile system. The relationship easily turns into one of considerable antagonism, and the more militant the pressure group, the greater the mutual antagonism.

To a greater or lesser degree, the same point holds for the relationship

[29] K. Newton, *Second City Politics* (1976), pp. 78–9.
[30] Ibid., p. 46.
[31] Ibid., p. 87. It is to be expected that senior officials should find it easier to consort with middle-class professionals and businessmen than with trade unionists and socialist activists. It is of some interest in this connection that, in Wolverhampton, essentially anti-socialist organizations like the Rotary and Round Table, founded in the 1920s, should have had as members chief officers like the Town Clerk, the Treasurer, the Chief Constable, the Medical Officer of Helath, and the Director of Education. (Jones, *Borough Politics*, pp. 135–6.) The organizations provided a social meeting-ground for these senior officials and anti-socialist councillors, and both no doubt felt this to be perfectly proper because the organizations were 'non-political'.

of Labour councillors to left activists in their own party. Faced with criticism and pressure from such activists, and indeed from left Labour colleagues in the Labour group on the council, 'moderate' councillors may well feel that they have more in common with their urbane and 'reasonable' Conservative counterparts in the council than with loud, 'irresponsible', and 'unrealistic' activists. Labour groups, or at least their 'moderate' majorities, have often made it one of their prime tasks to curb their militant colleagues, impose strict discipline upon them, and withstand the pressure of local activists in the constituency party, or outside it. Here, as in other contexts, oligarchical tendencies are not simply to be explained in terms of the 'inherent' nature of organization, or only as a means of protecting power and privilege: they are, to a large extent, the means whereby people set in deeply entrenched ideological and political positions seek to meet challenges to these positions.[32]

Ultimately, it is in the realm of ideology that the answer must be found to the question why Labour councils have not given more trouble to central government, and thus used their position at least to embarrass it. Given all the crippling penalties which are attached to it, persistent defiance is not something that councillors could be expected to resort to readily. But there is a range of possibilities between ready compliance and persistent defiance: Labour councils have not on the whole been keen to explore these possibilities. Keith-Lucas and Richards recall George Lansbury saying, when he was leading the struggle in Poplar in the early twenties, that 'we are all clear class-conscious Socialists working together, using the whole machinery of local government and Parliament for the transformation of Capitalist Society into Socialism. We are under no delusion about our day by day work. We are only patching up and making good some of the evils of Capitalism.'[33] This is not at all the spirit in which most Labour councils have approached their tasks. 'The prevailing ethos for most local Labour groups', it has been said, 'has not been "Poplarism", but what might be called Morrisonian aldermanic socialism, which merely follows in the traditions of the various "Improvement" parties of the mid-nineteenth century.'[34]

[32] For an interesting account of the process in one local authority, see D. G. Green, *Power and Party in an English City* (1981).

[33] Keith-Lucas and Richards, *History of Local Government*, p. 69.

[34] Bulpitt, *Party Politics*, p. 9. Mr Bulpitt also writes that 'before the First World War and during the 1920s, Labour candidates placed great emphasis on raising Public Assistance rates and Corporation wages, extending municipal trading (a Liberal policy to begin with), Direct Works, and municipal housing. But with a few exceptions such policies were geared to what would be accepted

As an ideology, Labourism has been much too weak, and too greatly lacking in a 'hegemonic' vocation, to sustain those who have subscribed to it against the great pressures which have been discussed earlier.

To those pressures may be added some others of equally great weight. Save in traditionally strong Labour enclaves, Labour councillors tend to operate in a climate of thought and politics dominated by conservative forces, and to be constantly in danger of attacks by these forces for extravagance, incompetence, wastefulness, and profligacy; and they are scarcely immune from such charges even in strongly Labour areas. The vast majority of the working-class electorate is altogether uninvolved in the business of the local authority in between elections, and the larger part of it cannot even be persuaded to vote at election time.[35] As a mobilizing agency, the Labour Party, nationally and at local level, has always been very weak; and the support which left-wing pressure groups may give to Labour councillors at election time is not particularly welcome. This is scarcely the climate in which a determination to face whatever odds in opposing the central government is likely to develop and be sustained. Nor, when there has been defiance, has the rebel authority been able to rely on the support of the national party. On the contrary, Labour leaders have found rebellious councils a great political embarrassment. Whether in office or in opposition, they have been the consistent advocates of compliance, and have strongly discouraged Labour authorities from seeking to tread any other path.

It is not therefore very difficult to understand why the relations of all governments with Labour councils have on the whole been smooth: the ideological dispositions of these authorities ensured that it should be so. Even so, there have been a good many cases over the years when a more radical attitude on the part of Labour councils has quickly turned local government into a terrain of quite fierce conflict; and such

---

by the central government.' (Ibid., p. 8.) The biographers of Herbert Morrison note that he was strongly opposed, as Mayor of Hackney, to the 'direct action' of the Poplar councillors, and that he proclaimed himself, with the great bulk of organized labour, as an adherent of 'democratic constitutionalism' (B. Donoughue and G. W. Jones, *Herbert Morrison, Portrait of a Politician* (1973), p. 47).

[35] The account previously cited of Clay Cross Council's resistance to the Government in the early seventies notes, in a significant observation, that 'there had been Labour councillors on Clay Cross Urban District, and at various times they had controlled the council. But councillors then tended to be people who were thought of as rather different from most; there was a feeling that they were something special, properly educated, that they understood finance.' (Skinner and Langdon, *Clay Cross*, p. 17.)

occasions have become more frequent in recent years, given the determination of central government to cut expenditure and services.

In this part of the political system as in all others, the application of greater and more forceful pressure from below produces strains and tensions which raise very large questions for capitalist democracy. It is with these questions that the final chapter is concerned.

6. THE FUTURE OF CAPITALIST DEMOCRACY IN BRITAIN

The question raised by the previous chapters is whether the British political system will in the future be able to contain as effectively as it has done in the past the pressures which are generated in society; or whether, because of the intensity and extent of these pressures, it will undergo fundamental change, and if so, in what directions. Another way of formulating the same question is to ask whether capitalist democracy in Britain can be expected to go on functioning as it has done over the last hundred years or so, and particularly since 1945.

The same sort of question has occasionally been asked about the British system ever since the extension of the suffrage, but it was asked in a context which made the questioning much less appopriate than it appears to be today. The extension of the suffrage and the arrival of 'the masses' on the political scene inspired fears about what 'democracy' might do, but Britain in the last third of the nineteenth century was an expanding and successful country, whose supremacy was not yet under challenge, and whose political system was sufficiently solid and secure to give confidence that it could absorb any pressures that the extended suffrage and any other development might generate. The context was somewhat less favourable in later periods, such as the years immediately preceding and those immediately following the First World War; but the British decline was still sufficiently relative and slow, and the material and psychological reserves still sufficiently ample (not least because large parts of Asia and Africa were still ruled by Britain) to make it possible for the mechanisms of containment in political and social life to operate without any undue difficulty.

The economic and social context is obviously much less favourable now, given continued and accelerated decline; the incapacity of successive governments, Labour as well as Conservative, to do much about it; the steady deterioration of the social fabric because of the systematic impoverishment of social and collective services that were never adequate in the first place; the decay of the inner cities allied to the vandalism of 'developers' in complicity with central and local government; the growth of social and racial tensions; the return of mass unemployment; and a generalized sense of uncertainty, insecurity, and resentment. The list could be extended;[1] and it does not seem pointless,

[1] One of its items would certainly be the character of the British prison system and the conditions in Britain's prisons.

in these circumstances, to ask whether the political system can continue
to protect this social order in more or less the same way as it has done
in the past.

There are in effect three possible answers to the question. The first is
that the political system will indeed be able to contain the pressures
to which it is subjected, and continue to function effectively, though
no doubt with some modifications which would not affect its basic
character. The second is that containment will require a continuing
tightening-up of the machinery of repression, to the point where the
political system, even if it retains its formal constitutional trappings,
nevertheless comes to be fundamentally different in its essential spirit
and mode of functioning. This means movement towards a 'strong
state' and a conservative-authoritarian regime. The third possibility
is that pressure from below would produce a government of the left
which, unlike the post-war Labour governments (not to speak of the
two minority pre-war ones), would seek to put into practice a far-
reaching socialist programme. This too would in all likelihood greatly
affect the workings and character of the political system.

Before these alternatives are considered further, something must
first be said about the meaning of political crisis and political change.

In one sense, political 'crises' and political change are almost daily
occurrences in capitalist democracies: a minister resigns or is dismissed;
a government is in difficulties, resigns, and is replaced by another; and
so on. This is the stuff of daily journalism, and is given exaggerated
importance by professional commentators who live by it. In fact, these
happenings are most often of no great consequence to anyone except
the actors themselves. The basic plot of the play remains the same,
even though some of the lines, and some of the actors, may be changed.

Sometimes, a good deal more may be at stake, and the consequences
of a set of events may be much larger, and the notion of crisis may then
have more meaning. The year 1931 produced a political crisis whose
outcome thrust the Labour Party into opposition, and gave to the
Conservative Party an overwhelming parliamentary preponderance
throughout the thirties, with disastrous consequences. Even here,
however, there was no *crisis of the regime* at all, and no change of any
significance in the way the political system functioned. Another example
of a major political crisis which was not a crisis of the regime is the
Suez fiasco, which led to the resignation of a prime minister, shook
Britain for a few weeks, and may have affected some policy orientations,
but had no other great impact.

Political crisis and political change may thus occur and produce

nothing in the way of a crisis of the regime, when the whole political system itself, and quite often the social system as well, come under serious challenge. The emergence of the Social Democratic Party in 1981 provides a recent example of a political development which, if the party were to prosper, could produce some considerable changes in political life; yet which would leave the basic character of the political system, and of the social order, quite untouched. The founding of a serious third party, much better able than the Liberal Party has been to challenge the predominance of the Labour and Conservative parties, would undoubtedly affect the workings of the political system: it would increase the likelihood of parliaments in which no single party had an absolute majority, and therefore of coalition politics, with all the manœuvrings this entails; it might also increase the vulnerability of governments to defeat in the House of Commons; it might increase the role of the monarch; and it would have a considerable impact on the Conservative and Labour parties.

All this is not insignificant; all the same, it would not transform the nature of the political system. Nor does the SDP pose the slightest threat to the existing structure of power and privilege in Britain. The formation of the party marks the logical outcome of the long battle which Roy Jenkins and other 'revisionists' in the Labour Party fought in the fifties under the leadership of Hugh Gaitskell to purge it of its traditional socialist commitments. The SDP is an explicitly anti-socialist party: its establishment as a strong factor in British politics would mean an access of strength to existing anti-socialist forces. Far from presenting a threat to the prevailing class system, it would provide an additional means of defence for it. The 'radical centre' which some of its progenitors proclaim as its vocation is but another, very familiar, version of reform-minded conservatism. In so far as the SDP may help to weaken the left, the political changes which it would bring about in political life would be favourable to the maintenance of the status quo, rather than detrimental to it.

Governments in capitalist democracies are also constantly subjected to innumerable pressures of every kind; and the political system usually absorbs them with greater or lesser ease, and with no crisis of the regime. One of the most notable features of capitalist democracy is precisely how resilient it is, and how great is the capacity of the political system to absorb crisis, conflict, and dislocation. Since 1945 there have been very few occasions in such regimes when pressures have been sufficiently strong to erupt into a crisis of the regime. Since the Second World War, only France, of major capitalist democracies, has experienced

such crises. The first was in 1958, when the inability of the Fourth Republic to bring the Algerian war to an end, coming on top of defeat in Indo-China, brought about its downfall. Even then, the Gaullism of the Fifth Republic turned out to be another version of capitalist democracy. The second occasion was in 1968, when it seemed for a short while that Gaullism itself might be toppled.

Nowhere else in major capitalist democracies has the regime faced this kind of threat. The United States, for example, was able to absorb the turmoil of the sixties, the crises over Vietnam, Watergate, and the resignation of a President, without any major (or even minor) impairment of the functioning of the political and constitutional system.

In Britain, there has been no crisis of the regime in this century. As I noted in Chapter 4, Ulster and Home Rule caused a serious political crisis in the years before the First World War; but it was much less serious and profound than appeared to many of the protagonists at the time. Nor did the combination of the crisis over Ulster with the other manifestations of the 'strange death of liberal England' – the struggle over the House of Lords, labour unrest, and the suffragette movement – amount to a crisis of the regime. It is also clear in retrospect that the fears expressed in high places in 1919 were not justified: Labour had no wish (or the capacity) to provoke a major crisis. Nor was there such a crisis in 1926, or at any time thereafter. It is in fact not too much to say that there has been no crisis of the regime in Britain since 1688, which is a long time. This is in no way conclusive as to what might happen in the future: immunity from revolutionary upheaval in the past, however long-lasting, is no immunity from revolutionary upheaval in the future. All the same, it does invite caution about predictions as to its likelihood in the near future. A great deal would have to happen in Britain before the prospect appeared in the least realistic.

Dangerous pressures upon a political system, capable of producing a crisis of the regime, may arise from different circumstances. Defeat in war is one such circumstance. Another is a regime's inability to resolve a major and particular problem, as was the case of France in Algeria. It is very doubtful, however, that continued failure by Britain to achieve a settlement in Ulster could produce a major crisis, however injurious its impact on Britain itself no doubt is, not to speak of the impact of such continued failure on Ulster. Again, nationalist demands, and notably the demand for secession, clearly have a powerful explosive potential. But it does not at present appear that Scottish nationalism, let alone its much weaker counterpart in Wales, will come to threaten the 'break-up' of Britain. A strong Scottish commitment to independence,

backed by a determined and well-based secessionist movement, would certainly produce a major crisis: but this seems very unlikely to come into being. Anything less dramatic is susceptible to accommodation.[2]

For Britain, it would seem that by far the most important source of crisis, in the strong sense of the term, must be taken to be continued economic decline, and the persistent inability of governments to resolve or attenuate in any substantial way the many economic and social problems which form part of the British scene. It is in this realm that the roots of constant, aggravated, cumulative, and ultimately 'destabilising' pressure lie.

The main *agency* of pressure from below will continue to be the working class: first, in the form of organized labour; and secondly in the form of voters. It must be added at once that there are many other agencies of pressure in British society, in the subordinate class and out of it: unemployed youths, black and white, irrupting with considerable force on the political scene, as in the riots of the summer of 1981; the women's movement; immigrant groups; movements for nuclear disarmament; and many others. Any such group or movement can make an impact on policy, and effect changes in what a government does. But no such group or movement can have anything like the impact of organized labour if it chooses to deploy and use its potential strength. Other agencies of pressure may bring about a measure of social and political change, or cause a political crisis: but it is organized labour alone which can provoke a major crisis capable of shaking a government and a regime.

However, pressure from organized labour can obviously be exercised for decade after decade, as it has done in Britain and all other major capitalist democracies, without producing such a crisis. I noted in Chapter 1 that pressure from labour is inherent in the capitalist mode of production, and that this includes a multitude of different objectives from better wages, shorter hours, and better conditions, to larger demands; and that such pressures can also assume a multitude of forms, from an isolated strike in one industry to a national strike across all industries. But all this constitutes part of the 'normal' pattern of life in capitalist society, and provides some of the 'raw material' to be processed by the political system. It must be taken for granted that pressure of this sort will continue to be generated; that objective conditions, even on the most favourable view, will continue to generate grievances and demands; and that the resistance of capital and the state

[2] For a different view, see T. Nairn, *The Break-Up of Britain* (London, 2nd edn., 1981).

to this pressure will continue to make for industrial and political conflict on a more or less continuous basis.

No doubt, the return of mass unemployment, first under a Labour government, and then, in a dramatically more accentuated form, under a Conservative one, has affected the intensity of this pressure. Mass unemployment produces a climate of fear and demoralization; increases competition for jobs; enhances 'sectionalism'; and reduces militancy. Conservsely, it strengthens the hand of the employers, enhances managerial authority, and reaffirms the dependence of the workers on the masters of the economy, who hold the key to the world of work. It is, in this sense, a daily defeat for labour.

In the inter-war years mass unemployment, allied to such defeats as the General Strike and the circumstances of the fall of the Labour Government in 1931, created conditions in which the larger part of the working class went through the thirties in a state of submission, resignation, and apathy. The post-war history of the working class, until recently, has on the contrary been marked by substantial gains at the 'point of production' and beyond; and while mass unemployment may weaken labour, it cannot erase the memory of past successes or reproduce the submissiveness of a long-gone era.

I have called this state of mind of the post-war working class a 'state of desubordination', in which 'people who find themselves in subordinate positions, and notably the people who work in factories, mines, offices, shops, schools, hospitals, and so on, do what they can to mitigate, resist and transform the conditions of their subordination'.[3] Desubordination is by no means based on socialist or revolutionary consciousness, and it may not even have much to do with 'class consciousness' in any precise way. No doubt many people do acquire such consciousness in the struggles in which they are engaged. But the important point here is that pressure is generated, and may be generated on a very large scale, by people who do not have much class or socialist consciousness, and whose demands and struggles are inspired by what Lenin called 'trade-union consciousness'. This latter consciousness has tended to be treated on the left as of no great consequence, and as a not very significant stage on the way to higher and better things. But there have been many instances in which a set of very specific, partial, 'economistic', and 'trade-union' demands have had a very considerable impact on the political process, even though the people engaged in struggles for these demands had no revolutionary consciousness or objectives. The miners'

[3] R. Miliband, 'A State of Desubordination', in *British Journal of Sociology*, xxix (1978) (4), 402.

strike in the winter of 1972–3 is a case in point. So is the earlier campaign against the Wilson Government's proposals of 1968–9 for curbs on strike action. Certainly, there are very definite limits to demands and campaigns inspired by 'trade-union consciousness': but such consciousness can nevertheless produce major problems for the political system.

Account must also be taken in this context of the lessened capacity of trade-union leaders, in comparison with, say, fifty years ago, to control and contain left activists in their unions. These activists can now be much less easily isolated from the rank and file than used to be the case; and the state of desurbordination of the rank and file gives greater currency to the message which the activists seek to convey.

Furthermore, 'organized labour' must now be taken to include a vast number of people in teaching and other forms of communication: here is to be found, for the first time in British history, an 'intellectual proletariat' which is insecure and often disaffected. Its contribution to the political culture of labour is already considerable and is likely to grow further.

The prospect, therefore, is one of continued conflict, antagonistic 'industrial relations', and a climate in which co-operation between the 'two sides of industry' remains as elusive as ever, notwithstanding the objurgations of politicians, prelates, and princes. Strike action is an habitual feature of such a situation, and episodically assumes the character of major and 'destabilizing' confrontations between labour and the state. Mass unemployment may help reduce militancy, but cannot stifle it. Nor can it transform a spirit of conflict into one of co-operation. Governments may seek a 'social contract' with the unions, or 'wage restraint', or an 'incomes policy'; but these endeavours are themselves sources of conflict. The simple fact is that genuine co-operation is not to be had in a class-based society such as Britain. British unions are not strong enough, by themselves, to dictate terms to employers and the state; but they are too strong to be forced into co-operation.

I noted earlier that this is the 'normal' pattern of life in capitalist democracy. But 'normality' can assume very different forms. In conditions of decline, growing and unresolved economic and social problems, generalized *malaise* and resentment, and constant pressure from labour and other sources, the temptation, for the people in charge of the state, is to strengthen its repressive side, and to seek a reduction in the capacity which exists in society for the effective manifestation of that pressure. Democratic forms increasingly come to be seen as a major problem — indeed as *the* major problem. For they make possible the

expression of excessive popular expectations and demands, and there-fore cause a dangerous 'overload' on the governmental system. Thus, Samuel Brittan writes that 'to escape from our predicament, we need not another revolution in economic theory, but a revolution in consti-tutional and political ideas which will save us from the *snare of unlimited democracy*, before we find ourselves with no democracy — and very little freedom — left'.[4]

Others of the same disposition go further; and it is worth noting how wholehearted is the approval of respectable intellectuals and commen-tators for restrictiveness and containment. For Maurice Cowling, writing in 1978, 'it is not freedom that Conservatives want; what they want is the sort of freedom that will maintain existing inequalities or restore lost ones, so far as political action can do this;[5] while Peregrine Wors-thorne, in an essay in the same volume entitled 'Too Much Freedom', also states that 'the urgent need today is for the state to regain control over "the people", to reassert its authority; and it is useless to imagine that this will be helped by some libertarian mish-mash drawn from the writings of Adam Smith, John Stuart Mill, and the warmed-up milk of nineteenth century liberalism'.[6] Clearly, some stronger inspiration, drawn from more tough-minded seers, is required. In a not dissimilar vein, one also finds Professor Robin Marris, as 'someone returning from five years abroad' (i.e. from the US, to take up a Chair of Economics at Birkbeck College), offering 'some thoughts' in an article in *The Times* to the delegates to the Social Democratic Party Conference at the

---

[4] S. Brittan, 'The Economic Consequences of Democracy', in R. Skidelsky (ed.), *The End of the Keynesian Era* (1977), p. 49 (my italics). Note also his view that the 'two endemic threats' to liberal representative democracy are 'a) the generation of excessive expectations; and b) the disruptive effect of the pursuit of group self interest in the market place' ('The Economic Contradictions of Democracy', in *British Journal of Political Science* (1975), v (pt. II), 129).

[5] M. Cowling, 'The Present Crisis', in M. Cowling (ed.), *Conservative Essays* (1978), p. 9. In the same essay Mr Cowling writes that 'the Conservative Party exists now, as at any time since 1886, because those who perform the duties or acquire the benefits connected with inequality, do not want democratic arrange-ments to break down. They judge it better, it possible, to get part of what they want by acting effectively through the parliamentary system than to get a bigger proportion under some other sort of regime. They accept the fact that a balancing of costs is involved and that, if the price that is paid for parliamentary govern-ment is too high, there will be those who will want parliamentary arrangements superseded.' (Ibid., p. 16.)

[6] P. Worsthorne, 'Too much Freedom', in ibid., p. 149. Mr Worsthorne also made a notable contribution to the literature produced by the riots of the summer of 1981. There way no way, he wrote, of ameliorating the lot of the inner cities; therefore, 'better the reactionary callousness that angers than the progressive compassion that demeans; *better heads cracked by a policeman's truncheon than souls swamped by society's pity*' (*Sunday Telegraph*, 12 July 1981. My italics).

beginning of October 1981; the nature of these thoughts is sufficiently indicated by the title of the article — 'Why the SDP should abolish the right to strike' — and by his remark that 'the right to strike is become as anti-social as the gun'.[7]

Sentiments of this kind are quite common; and they point to a conservative rage directed against the left, the trade unions, activists, dissidents, even 'liberals' and other such inadequately tough-minded people. In deteriorating economic circumstances, and in conditions of heightened class conflict, it must be expected that the emphasis on law and order, stability, the curbing of strikes, and the stifling of activism, would all find much support, and make possible a much harsher version of capitalist democracy than has been experienced in Britain so far.

It is somewhere along this path that lies the second alternative to which I referred at the beginning of this chapter, namely the transformation of capitalist democracy into a conservative-authoritarian regime. It is a mistake to think that such a transformation must necessarily involve a sharp break from one stage to another: what may be involved is a gradual slide — the peaceful transition, relatively speaking, from capitalist democracy to capitalist authoritarianism.

Nor is there only one form of authoritarianism. If 'it can't happen here' is meant to refer to Fascism as it was experienced in Italy or Germany, it is almost certainly right to say that it cannot happen here. But it is not very difficult to conceive of a British form of conservative authoritarianism, which would maintain some of the features of traditional constitutionalism, proclaim its dedication to ultimately democratic objectives, assure one and all that the state of emergency would not last a day longer than necessary, and insist that the measures taken under that state of emergency, though no doubt drastic, were clearly essential for national recovery and renewal. The script is very familiar and can, in suitable circumstances, be used anywhere.

In such a regime, trade unions might be allowed, provided they did not organize strikes. Parties might operate, provided they were not subversive. Political activity might be possible, provided permission had been obtained for it. Newspapers would be allowed, provided they did not foment 'class hatred' or 'spread disaffection'. Comment on radio and television would be free, provided it did not undermine stability. There would be censorship, but on a limited basis: on the other hand, self-censorship would be unlimited.

[7] *The Times*, 5 October 1981.

Soldiers would play a much bigger role in all areas of national life than hitherto, but the regime would not necessarily be a military one. There would be plenty of civilians, of the most respectable hue, available to run the state, in partnership with military men and police chiefs. Police forces would be given much more extensive powers, and much more of a free hand to act as they thought fit. Nor, in the climate engendered by the regime and its propagandists, would they be disposed to ask anyone's permission to do so.

Nevertheless, much of the state would function more or less normally. A dismal aspect of such conservative authoritarianism is precisely the normality which endures, and which provides reassurance to many people who want a quiet life that things are not all that different, really, except of course for activists and others in gaol or rehabilitation centers of one sort of another ('concentration camp' evokes the wrong memories). There would be cricket on the green, and at Lord's; Derby Day at Ascot; the football season and the FA Cup; comedy on television; the same announcers blandly reading the news; the Queen's Christmas Broadcast; even the House of Commons, minus some unpatriotic MPs, temporarily detained.

There would certainly be resistance, from the left and the labour movement, and also beyond it. But this would itself be taken by many people to justify the repressive measures taken against trouble-makers and subversives, and would serve to justify further measures of repression. It would not be realistic to underestimate the degree of support which such a regime, coming in after a prolonged period of instability and conflict, would enjoy from all conservative forces in the country – in the press,[8] from industry, commerce, and finance, from members of the academic community and many other intellectuals, in the professions, from many patriotic associations, from many church leaders. The support would no doubt be qualified and even critical in many cases; but that would do well enough.

Nor would the regime lack friends abroad. It would of course be violently anti-Communist and strongly committed to Cold War policies. It would therefore be able to rely on the sympathetic understanding of the United States, and of many other countries as well.

[8] It is worth recalling here that the day after Salvador Allende was overthrown by a military coup in Chile (and assassinated), *The Times* had an editorial on the coup which said that 'whether or not the armed forces were right to do what they have done, the circumstances were such that *a reasonable military man could in good faith have thought it his constitutional duty to intervene*' (*The Times*, 13 September 1973). The Editor of *The Times* was then William (now Sir William) Rees-Mogg.

This kind of projection is easily dismissed as a sign of pronounced paranoia. But I doubt that it is. Certainly, there is a long way to go before any such projection comes to be realized; and it may well never be. But it is just as well to see how far things have already gone; and also to note that the state is well equipped, by way of such enactments as the Emergency Powers Acts and the Prevention of Terrorism Acts, to wield the most extraordinary powers, strictly within the framework of constitutionalism. Under the former, the cabinet is empowered to draw up regulations and to assume such powers and duties as it deems necessary for the restoration of order and the maintenance of supplies, or for any other purpose – the only check upon it, such as it is, being the requirement that the regulations be renewed at regular intervals by Parliament. Since its first promulgation in 1920 (strictly speaking in 1914), emergency legislation has been invoked by both Conservative and Labour governments to deal with major strikes, and is available for any crisis. The Prevention of Terrorism (Temporary Provisions) Acts of 1974 and 1976, directed mainly at IRA terrorist activities in Britain, empowered the Home Secretary to ban organizations which appeared to him to be concerned with terrorism, to exclude from Britain any person he believed to have been involved in the 'commission, preparation or instigation' of acts of terrorism, and, most important of all, gave the police the power to arrest without warrant and to hold in custody for a number of days persons believed to be terrorist suspects. These Acts are specifically directed at IRA terrorism in Britain: no doubt, variants of them directed at very different activities could be formulated.

My argument is simply that, in sharply deteriorating conditions and in circumstances of exacerbated class conflict, the 'strong state', in some suitably British form, and with pronounced authoritarian features, is not impossible, and is prefigured by the widening ambit of repressive state power; and that the coming of such a state would be greeted with much approval by many important people, and by many 'ordinary' people as well. To argue that the 'strong state' is already here, more or less, is wrong. To think that its coming is inevitable is dangerously pessimistic, and ignores all the forces which make its coming less likely. To think that it could never come would be dangerously complacent.

Beside the pressure from organized labour, the other major source of pressure from below in Britain would be the endorsement by working-class and other voters, as on previous occasions, of a programme of radical reform, as a result of which a government pledged to carry out such a programme would be returned with an adequate parliamentary

majority. This is the third of the possibilities mentioned at the beginning of this chapter, and the one envisaged and hoped for by much of the left, both within and outside the Labour Party.

One assumption on which this 'scenario' is based, to my mind very reasonably, is that, in conditions of capitalist democracy, no other path for the achievement of power is open. So long as the achievement of a parliamentary majority appears possible, so long must any alternative strategy, based upon the expectation of a revolutionary seizure of power, remain of very marginal political significance. No such seizure of power is conceivable without substantial popular support: but no such popular support for insurrectionary purposes is to be had in conditions of capitalist democracy. This turns the insurrectionary project into a fantasy.

This is not to say that a major reorganization of capitalist society in socialist directions can necessarily be achieved by way of a parliamentary majority: all it means is that any other strategy commands no serious support. Of course, the transformation of capitalist democracy into capitalist authoritarianism would create an entirely different set of circumstances and produce different perspectives and strategies.

A second assumption which is made by the left − or much of the left − in Britain is that the changes it wants will be brought about by a Labour government. This requires further probing.

What is involved here is not only the *adoption* by the Labour Party of a far-reaching programme of socialist reform at home and a major shift in orientations abroad: the *carrying out* of such a programme by a Labour government is also involved.

There are strong reasons for thinking that this is a very unlikely prospect. It is not inconceivable that a Labour government, much on the pattern of previous ones, and dominated by people in the Attlee–Gaitskell–Wilson–Callaghan mould, could again happen, even though the prospect of such a government, with a majority, has become much more doubtful because of the Labour Party's divisions and the emergence of the Social Democratic Party. But even if it did come into being, its domination by the centre and right of the Labour parliamentary leadership would ensure that it did not seek to bring about the kind of changes which the left demands.

Such a government would be different, in many of its policies and in all of its tone, from that of Mrs Thatcher's Conservative Government. It would repeal the legislation against trade unions which that Government has placed on the statute book − or at least a good deal of that legislation. And it would no doubt do many other things which are

badly wanted by the labour movement and beyond. This is why many people on the left, who want a lot more, are willing to settle for less, on the principle that half a loaf is better than no bread, and that even a crust of bread is better than the fare which has been on offer since the Conservative Government came to office in May 1979.

This is of course a very different argument from the one noted earlier, and according to which fundamental transformations in socialist directions, rather than some limited reforms, are possible through the Labour Party as it now is. It is this argument which invites the greatest scepticism. For it ignores or greatly underscores the very large fact that many if not most of the people who would occupy the senior positions in a Labour government, and who would generally dominate it, do not *believe* in the basic items of the socialist left's programme, and are in fact profoundly, even passionately, opposed to these items.

Thus, socialists want the appropriation into the public domain of the 'commanding heights' of the economy, not least its financial heights. But this has always been, and remains, anathema to the Labour right and centre. Similarly, socialists take very seriously the pledge of the Labour Party's programme of 1973, enshrined in its Election Manifesto in Februrary 1974, to bring about 'a fundamental and irreversible shift in the balance of power and wealth in favour of working people and their families'. But there is not the slightest reason to believe that a future Labour government, dominated by the same kind of people who were in charge between 1974 and 1979 (indeed many of them the same people) would address itself to the task with any greater zeal than was the case in the years gone by.

Also, the socialist left wants some major reorientations in defence and foreign policy, including measures such as the closing down of United States nuclear bases in Britain and other measures of unilateral disarmament: but this would run gravely counter to the commitment to NATO and the American alliance which has been the very corner-stone of Labour's defence and foreign policies since the Second World War.

On every major item of policy advocated by the left, there is either total disagreement by the Labour right and centre, or a critical difference of approach and emphasis. This only reflects a division which is as old as the Labour Party itself, between those who view it as a vehicle of reform within the existing social order and those who view it as a vehicle for the socialist transformation of that social order. This division may not make it impossible for the Labour Party to adopt a programme sufficiently ambiguous for everyone to find in it what he or she wants, but even if the Labour Party were to win a General Election on that

programme, the Labour government that would then be formed would include, in offices of great power and influence, men and women who would take it to be a crucial part of their duty to defeat or defuse such socialist proposals as might make their way to the cabinet's agenda; and they would do this with the clearest conscience, given their conviction that these proposals were dangerous and ill-conceived.

It is not realistic to think that a programme of great changes, of the sort wanted by the left, could be implemented under such conditions. Such a programme is in any case bound to be very difficult to carry out. Powerful forces would obviously be opposed to one or other part of it, or more likely to all of it. Industry, commerce, and finance, and their many friends abroad; the Conservative and other anti-socialist parties and groupings; lobbies and associations of every description; most of the press and other organs of opinion; many professional people in all walks of life — all would want to do what was in their power to bring about the paralysis and defeat of the government. Nor would the government be able to rely on much support from within the state itself; on the contrary, there would be great hostility to what the government was trying to do on the part of senior civil servants, officers in the armed forces, police chiefs, judges, the House of Lords, Court circles. What precisely they would do in practice is uncertain: but there is nothing uncertain about the hostility which they would feel towards a government bent, in their eyes, on utterly catstrophic courses.

This opposition would not be conclusive; but the first condition for it not to be conclusive is that the government itself should be united, resolute, clear in purpose. A divided, uncertain, and incoherent government is not a fit instrument to engineer a social revolution. But a divided, uncertain, and incoherent government is the best which the Labour Party, in its present condition, is able to produce. This has nothing to do with the personal qualities of the people concerned: it is rather the result of the ideological dispositions of the men and women in effective charge of the Labour Party. They may want reform, but do not want a social revolution on any terms, and conceive it to be their duty, as did their predecessors, to block the path of those who do.

In this endeavour they may expect to achieve a fair measure of success. But they are rather less likely to achieve a reversal of the decline in support which the Labour Party, under the guidance of the right and centre, has suffered since 1951. In the General Election of that year Labour obtained nearly 14,000,000 votes (48.8 per cent). In the General Election of 1964 it was down to 12,206,000 (44.1 per cent). It regained some ground in the General Election of 1966 —

13,065,000 (47.9 per cent); but fell to 11,510,000 votes in 1979 (36.9 per cent). The decline cannot, strictly speaking, be described as disastrous, but it has nevertheless been very marked; and it clearly signifies that Labour has been quite unable to gain support among large numbers of people, in the working class and beyond, to whom it should have been able to appeal. Nor has the Labour Party been able to retain the mass membership it had in the post-war years. It could claim more than a million individual members in 1951: by the beginning of the eighties, its individual membership was down to less than one-third of that figure.

The reason for Labour's electoral and political decline cannot be attributed to any profound shift to Conservatism, but rather to the fact that people whom Labour ought to attract find nothing to inspire them in the prospect of a Labour government, and this stems largely from the performance of the Labour governments of the sixties and seventies. But the Labour Party, under its present management, has nothing more to offer than an updated version of those performances.

Most of the people to whom Labour ought to appeal are not socialists; but there is no reason to think that they could not be persudaded to support a socialist programme offering a real hope of recovery and renewal, and presented to them with conviction and argument. This, however, is precisely the problem. For the Labour Party cannot now mobilize electoral and political support for socialist policies in which most of its leaders do not believe and to which they are implacably opposed.

Given the overwhelming preponderance which the Labour Party retains on the left, this also means that there is no major political force which can at present be said to offer the promise of an effective challenge to the existing structures of power in Britain: any such challenge must, at best, be rather weak and uncertain. How this is to be remedied is a matter of great contention among socialists; and it is also a matter of crucial importance. For a strong and unambiguous political force on the left is not only indispensable for the achievement of great economic and social changes: it is also essential for the purpose of opposing effectively the drift towards conservative authoritarianism.

INDEX

activism, 154; left-wing, 30, 54, 71
activist: minority, 12; presence in
unions, 63, 72; pressure, 40
activists, 14, 15, 24, 34, 39, 40, 41,
54, 64, 67, 68, 69, 70, 71, 72,
93, 112, 143, 155; Communist,
111; Conservative, 67, 68, 79;
grass-roots, 14, 67; harassment
of, 112; labour, 37, 75, 92; left-
wing, 13, 28, 42, 64, 65, 68, 95,
105, 111; local, 137, 143;
socialist, 29, 30; working-class,
13, 91
Advisory, Conciliation, and Arbitration Service, 59
Allende, Salvador, 155 n.8
American alliance, 81, 92, 158
Amery, Leo, 127 n.51
Anderson, Perry, 55
apparatus, military and police, 94.
See also military, military chiefs,
police, police chiefs
armed forces, 110
Arnold, Matthew, 88
artisans, 12
Asquith, Herbert, 30, 114, 114 n.27, 129
Atkins, Lord, 119
Attlee, Clement, 34, 81, 100, 102,
105, 157; Government, 17, 44,
100

Bagehot, Walter, 26, 40, 41, 69, 127
Baldwin, Stanley, 31, 32, 65 n.20,
79 n.38, 127
Balfour, Arthur, 3, 5
Bank of England, 8, 35; Governor
of, 108
Beira Patrol, 124 n.43
Benn, Tony, 43 n.42, 86, 107
Bevan, Aneurin, 41, 42, 43, 44, 86;
Bevanism, 46; Bevanite chal-
lenge, 45
Bevin, Ernest, 102
Bingham Report, 123
Black and Tans, 112 n.22
Blacks, 113, 150. *See also* coloured
immigrants
Blake, Robert, 5, 114, 114 n.27

Bloomsbury, 88
Bolshevik Revolution, 3, 73;
Bolshevism, 73, 73 n.32, 74, 79
British Broadcasting Corporation,
79, 80, 81, 83, 84
British Petroleum, 123, 124 n.43
British Union of Fascists, 48
Burnett, John, 56
Butler, R. A., 35, n.28

Cabinet, 17, 104, 106
Cadogan, Alexander, 105 n.10
Callaghan, James, 72 n.30, 157;
Callaghan Government, 60
Cambridge, 7, 88, 103, 116
Campaign for Labour Party Democracy, 72
capital, 94, 118
capitalist: authoritarianism, 154,
157; class, 6; countries, 83;
democracy, 1, 20, 38, 39, 77,
94, 97, 99, 112, 145, 146, 148,
149, 152, 154, 157; countries,
83; economy, 80; enterprise, 84,
85, 94, 95, 97, 103; mode of
production, 6, 77, 150; society,
6, 12, 150
Carlyle, Thomas, 102
Castle, Barbara, 102
Cecil, Lord Robert, 31
Central College, 13
central government, 134, 139, 140,
141, 144 n.34, 145
Chamberlain, Neville, 31, 43, 50,
51, 80 n.39
Chartism, 3, 22, 23, 24
Chile, 155 n.8
Christian Socialism, 88
Christianity, 88
churches, 78
Churchill, Randolph, 27 n.19
Churchill, Winston, 2 n.1, 37 n.35,
43, 44, 47, 49, 52, 80 n.39,
115, 115 n.30; Coalition Govern-
ment, 43
Citrine, Walter, 57
City, 8, 96; institutions, 8 n.10
class: analysis, 15; conflict, 4, 14,